Vuillard

Vuillard

Belinda Thomson

Abbeville Press · Publishers · New York

Front cover: Detail from *The 'Clos Cézanne' at Vaucresson*. Back cover: *In the Hessels' Salon, Evening, rue de Naples.*

First Abbeville Press edition, 1988
© Phaidon Press Limited, Oxford, 1988

Library of Congress Cataloging in Publication Data
Thomson, Belinda.
Vuillard / Belinda Thomson. — 1st ed.
p.   cm.
Bibliography : p.
Includes index.
ISBN 0-89659-883-7
1. Vuillard, Edouard. 1868–1940 — Criticism and interpretation.
2. Painting, French.   3. Painting, Modern — 20th century — France.
I. Title.
ND553.V9T48   1988
759.4 — dc19   88-6188
CIP

Printed in England by Ebenezer Baylis & Son Limited, Worcester

ACKNOWLEDGEMENTS

I would like to express my deep thanks to M. Antoine Salomon without whose support and trust this book would never have been written. Much of my information concerning Vuillard's life and work is based on unpublished material in M. Salomon's archive, which has been assembled over many years in preparation for the *catalogue raisonné* of Vuillard's *oeuvre*. Thanks to his generosity I have had access to invaluable transcripts of the artist's as yet unpublished journal, the original 48 manuscript volumes of which are deposited in the library of the Institut de France. The *catalogue raisonné* (forthcoming) is a major project. Originally undertaken after Vuillard's death by Jacques Salomon (married to the artist's niece Annette Roussel), the work on the catalogue has been carried forward since the 1950s by his son Antoine, with the assistance over a number of years of Juliet Wilson Bareau. I would like to thank the latter for her friendship, enthusiasm and unstinting help with my research queries and for reading the manuscript with painstaking care. While I have benefited greatly from being able to share with Antoine Salomon and Juliet Wilson Bareau the fruits of their knowledge of Vuillard and his *oeuvre*, any remaining errors of fact or interpretation are my responsibility alone.

Sincere thanks are also due to my editor, Penelope Marcus, whose vision and impatience saw the book through, to Denise Hardy and Peg Katritzky for picture research and to my copy-editor Diana Davies. Many other individuals, scholars, dealers and collectors, have helped me in different ways and I take this opportunity to thank them; Stanley Chapman, Peter Ferriday, Susan Foister, Thomas Gibson, Gloria Groom, Samuel, Paul and Ellen Josefowitz, Suzanne McCullagh, Jane Munro, Christian Neffe, Anna Gruetzner Robbins, Stephen Romer. I would also like to thank the many private collectors who have generously allowed me to reproduce their pictures, often for the first time. Last but by no means least, I am grateful to my husband and family for sustaining me through the joys and pains of writing this book.

(Half-title) *The Visitor. Annette in the rue de Calais Salon. c.* 1920. Pencil on paper, 5⅛ × 8½ in. (13 × 21.5 cm.). Private Collection

Frontispiece *Vallotton and Misia in the Dining-Room, rue Saint-Florentin*. Dated 1899. Oil on cardboard, 26¾ × 20 in. (67.7 × 50.6 cm.). William Kelly Simpson

CONTENTS

1 *A Man and Two Horses. c.* 1890. Oil on cardboard, 10⅞ × 13¾ in. (27.5 × 35cm.). Josefowitz Collection

INTRODUCTION

Few artists were so universally liked and admired during their lifetime as Edouard Vuillard. Today he continues to hold a special place in the affections of most lovers of the art of a period rich in talent and diversity. His sometimes bold, always subtle sense of colour harmonies, his feeling for textures and patterned shapes, his sure sense of pictorial structure are among the enduring qualities of his art. As a realist imbued with the aspirations of Symbolism he had a rare ability to evoke the atmosphere of an interior, to get beyond the superficial and penetrate the mysterious core of reality. In portraits his great gift was to catch the mood of his models during their most private unguarded moments. At the same time his ability to conceive decorations on a large scale, an ability fuelled by his experiences in the theatre, made Vuillard one of the foremost decorators of an era that saw the reinstatement of decorative painting as one of the highest achievements of the artist.

Vuillard's range of subject-matter was largely confined to the near at hand, the familiar, the modern and the everyday. This no longer strikes one as a limitation but as a commitment, shared by many of his contemporaries. Today one can applaud his integrity in remaining true to his realist origins while experimenting and taking risks at the formal level. When in 1890 the 'notion of the picture' was redefined by the Nabi aesthetic, and its traditional mimetic function opened to question, Vuillard responded to the challenge. He worked through the lesson of synthetism, painfully and with misgivings, producing along the way some of the most remarkably balanced, charged and simplified images of the Symbolist era. That initial period of reassessment and relearning provided the basis for his later development of a style of greater detail and richness, a style that corresponded more closely to his breadth and variety of vision.

Most recent assessments of Vuillard's career have placed great emphasis on the experimental works he produced early on and neglected or dismissed his later work. This imbalance and prejudice is reflected in the fact that like Bonnard, Vuillard has very often been categorized as an Intimist; the label describes his domestic interiors and portraits well enough, but ignores completely his achievements as a landscapist and as a decorator. Because of the diversity of his media and of his types of work, each phase of Vuillard's career offers interest both at the artistic level and at the level of social history. His later portraits and interiors, which mirrored as it were the lives of the rich and the less rich in the 1920s and 1930s, not always uncritically, are fascinating documents of the past. So too are his decorative schemes. The Nabis's greatest ambition was to be recognized as decorators and Vuillard's achievements in this area were unparalleled. Paradoxically, his decorations have remained the least-known aspect of his career. It requires an effort of imagination and reconstruction today to envisage them in their original settings and serving their original function. Several were altered from their first state by Vuillard himself in order to accord with a new setting or satisfy a new client; most of the larger series have been broken up and now hang out of context. It is time to reassess his importance in this field.

Hitherto Vuillard himself has been approached chiefly through the eyes of those who knew him. We have been presented with a calm, reserved, modest and gentle figure, devoted to his mother and beloved by his friends, an artist of exquisite sensitivity. Yet of Vuillard's own views we learnt very little. He remained a shadowy, self-effacing figure. Now at last a more balanced overview of Vuillard's achievements and artistic personality is beginning to emerge, and for the first time it is possible to hear him speak through his journal. This unique document, which remained inaccessible for forty years after his death and is still unpublished, reveals much about his day-to-day thinking and anxieties about his art, of the rich range of his reference to the work of other artists, writers, people and ideas, and something of the intelligence and energy that went into his working practice. With the aid of the journal we can begin to understand how his relationships with people and ideas – friends and family, earlier art, literature and drama – shaped and underscored the meaning of his works and the elaboration of his vast *oeuvre*.

Chapter One

VUILLARD THE REALIST: BACKGROUND AND ARTISTIC DÉBUT

According to his fellow Nabi and close friend Maurice Denis, Vuillard manifested an almost religious seriousness of purpose about his artistic vocation. Such single-minded professionalism was an ideal to which all the Nabis aspired when they first formed their secret brotherhood in 1888–9. It was probably on artists such as Puvis de Chavannes and, at a greater remove, Delacroix and Le Sueur, that Vuillard modelled his working life, career and ambitions. In Delacroix, Vuillard could find an artist of similarly emotional temperament, high ambition, wide culture, beset by shyness in society and by crippling moral scruples, whose refuge and calm lay in his regular and solitary working practices. The publication of Delacroix's *Journal*, the first volume of which appeared in 1893 under the supervision of René Piot, a contemporary and friend of Vuillard and the Nabis, provided an important intellectual stimulus for Vuillard's generation and became obligatory reading for the débutant artist. Vuillard's journal has distinct similarities with the *Journal* of Delacroix, being kept up intensively at first then abandoned for a period, only to be resumed more regularly at a later stage. The years 1888–90 and 1894 are densely covered, then there is a hiatus. He seems to have returned to making entries on a regular, sometimes daily, basis in 1907. Vuillard's journal was an outlet for the expression of feeling, self-examination and criticism, a more private, personal and confessional affair than the contemporary journals of either Maurice Denis or Paul Signac, both of whom wrote with a keener sense of history, and possibly in the expectation of publication. Like Delacroix, Vuillard would seem to have used words to clarify or germinate aesthetic, pictorial and technical ideas.

Quite apart from his frequently stated admiration for Puvis de Chavannes, Vuillard prided himself on having geographical links with him too. Both artists had their origins in Cuiseaux, a small town on the edge of the Jura where Vuillard's father, having retired as a marine infantry captain with the Légion d'Honneur, served for several years as tax collector. On both sides of the family – in fact, his mother Marie, née Michaud, had married her father's cousin, Honoré Vuillard – Vuillard had well-established roots in the Jura and returned to visit Cuiseaux on several occasions. Like Puvis in this respect, though unlike that other native of the Jura, Gustave Courbet, there was nothing provincial about Vuillard's appearance or behaviour, although he evidently inherited the reserved, reflective temperament and slowness of speech thought to be typical of his countrymen.

The youngest of three children, Vuillard was born on 11 November 1868. From the age of nine he lived in Paris, following his father's retirement. His mother, a Parisienne herself and considerably younger than her husband, joined a firm of corset-makers with premises near the Opéra, taking over the business and no doubt fashionable clientèle of a Mme Duval-Caron in 1879. By dint of hard work Mme Vuillard was able to make a reasonable living. After her husband's death in 1883 she moved the business into her own home and brought her only daughter Marie in to help when she was old enough. The seamstresses' workshop later provided Vuillard with inspiration for many a painting. The Vuillards' various Paris apartments, which doubled as workshops in the early years, give an impression of frugality and simplicity, the ritual of the family meal around a circular table providing the main diversion from the repeated needlework tasks associated with the business.

Vuillard never married, but remained close to his mother until her death in 1928. Despite a busy round of social engagements that later brought him into contact with a much more glamorous and moneyed society than he was used to, he never swerved from the modest existence of the *moyenne bourgeoisie* which he shared with her. It was undoubtedly Mme Vuillard's encouragement, thrift and industry that saw her son through his studies and provided the bedrock of income during his first impecunious years. Later Vuillard in his turn would provide for his mother's needs. Registering her familiar and solid image was perhaps one way for him to acknowledge all he owed to her equable good nature and devotion to his artistic career (Plates 2, 3).

Had Vuillard followed family tradition, he would have made a career either in the army, like his elder brother Alexandre, or in commerce. His mother's family had connections with the clothing industry, her aunt Caroline, Vuillard's godmother, having married Jean Saurel, a fabric designer. Vuillard's education in Paris began with a period of study with the Marist fathers, which some have argued established habits of mind of an almost Jansenist asceticism that Vuillard never threw off, after which he enjoyed the liberal education offered by the celebrated lycée Condorcet. The progressive, anti-clerical curriculum, coupled with the school's location in the Opéra quarter, with its theatres, publishers' offices and fashionable department stores, helped to ensure that its alert pupils emerged *au courant* with the latest trends in high and low art, popular and more elitist culture. Almost all of Vuillard's future Nabi associates attended this school and it formed the nucleus of journalists, poets, musicians and playwrights who would make up his immediate circle, many of them contributors to the literary journal *La Revue Blanche*. His closest friend at school was Ker-Xavier Roussel, son of a well-to-do and cultured doctor.

When Roussel and Vuillard left Condorcet in 1885, the former, already set on an artistic career, entered the studio of the 'Prix de Rome' Diogène Maillart, who was a regular exhibitor at the Salon. Vuillard was apparently preparing the entrance examination for the military college of Saint-Cyr when the enthusiastic persuasion of Roussel led him to enrol at Maillart's free evening classes at the Gobelins school. Whether, as has been frequently claimed, Vuillard had no previous inkling of a talent for drawing or inclination towards an artistic career seems dubious. His school exercise books and other unpublished early material reveal him to have been constantly making sketches, some of which he signed and dated. There are several explorations of classical and medieval themes among his unpublished student work, including the compositional drawing, *The Death of Caesar* (Plate 7), made in pen and wash, which deploys a neo-classical frieze arrangement of violently gesturing nude male figures.

In about 1908, Vuillard made a résumé in his journal of key events that had shaped his début as an artist. From the year 1887, when he was 19, he recalled his move from the rue du Marché Saint-Honoré to the rue de Miromesnil, and the following: 'Julian's intermittently. Still lifes for the dining room. Baudry. Stained glass collodions of Roussel's father. Accepted at the Ecole in July after 3 failures.' Vuillard had made his first unsuccessful attempt to pass the entrance examination for the Ecole des Beaux-Arts early in 1886. While preparing to resit the exams, he enrolled at the Académie Julian, where he could gain practice in drawing from the cast, from engravings and paintings of earlier masters and from the model, the teaching being compatible with academic teaching at the Ecole. On some academic nude studies Vuillard inscribed himself as 'pupil of

2 *Mme Vuillard in front of the Mirror.* 1900. Oil on cardboard, 19½ × 14 in. (49.5 × 35.5 cm.).
The Barber Institute of Fine Arts, The University of Birmingham

Messrs Bouguereau, Robert-Fleury and Gérôme', artists who taught at both institutions. The significance for Vuillard of stained-glass collodions and of Baudry is intriguing. Paul Baudry was best known for his large series of decorative paintings in Garnier's new Opera house which had been unveiled in 1874. Following his death in early 1886 a major retrospective of Baudry's *oeuvre* was held at the Ecole des Beaux-Arts, which Vuillard may well have seen.

In 1888 Vuillard noted in his journal 'passage at the Ecole, Gérôme 6 weeks', which suggests that his actual attendance at the Ecole was of very short duration. He was also attending the 'Cours Yvon et Montparnasse' and there are jottings relating to these geometry, perspective and anatomy classes. However, Vuillard's main artistic education was taking place in the Louvre, where he was an assiduous and receptive student. The first volume of the journal shows his progress through the different galleries and reveals his predilections for different artists almost day by day in the winter of 1888. In thumbnail sketches he noted works whose composition interested him as well as compositions of his own, usually still lifes or interiors, that he had recently completed or intended to pursue. His early enthusiasms were for Holbein, the Venetians Titian and Veronese, the Dutch seventeenth-century genre painters, and especially Rembrandt, and for the French eighteenth-century painters who were so closely linked to that tradition, notably Watteau and Chardin. One senses, from the tenor of his remarks about the Italians' love of 'rhetoric', that his obligatory periods of study in front of the revered masters of the Renaissance, Michelangelo, Leonardo and Raphael, were respectful rather than pleasurable. Vuillard seems to have used the word 'rhetoric' here in a pejorative sense, to denote the formulaic and mannered habits or tricks of representation characteristic of certain artists of the past. One of his greatest early obsessions was to avoid becoming 'rhetorical' himself.

In addition to these visits to the Louvre, Vuillard often recorded observations of Paris street life, the river, the theatre, and of his family's comings and goings; these tiny sketches lay the foundations, in miniature, of much work to come. A key preoccupation seems to have been the study of light effects, the silhouette of a figure in a doorway, reflections of shop windows on a wet pavement or the halo of brilliance around a lamp in an interior (Plate 8). To judge from the names of the contemporary artists he mentions, Vuillard as yet had no interest in the work of the Impressionists or Neo-Impressionists. Rather he was drawn to the work of Puvis de Chavannes and Albert Besnard. Besnard was a fashionable artist, admired in the late 1880s for his harnessing of broad, painterly handling, reminiscent of Manet, and a bright palette to the officially sanctioned range of portraits and decorative commissions that he undertook. He had just completed a series of decorations for the Salle des Mariages of the Mairie du Ier arrondissement which were praised by several critics for their symbolist mood and thoughtful revitalization of the age-old theme of the seasons. By 1894, however, Vuillard was able to note that he had the confidence to trust his own sensations before nature, and no longer tried to find the equivalents of the forms he saw in the work of an artist such as Besnard.

Vuillard's close artist friends at this time were Charles Cottet and Marc Mouclier. The former was to gain a reputation as a painter of Breton subjects; the latter had a less successful career as a painter of tonal interiors, still lifes and arcadian landscapes. Studio discussions with these friends lay behind the generalized naturalist aesthetic reflections that one meets in Vuillard's journal entry for 22 November 1888: 'We perceive nature through our senses, which give us images of forms and colours, sound, etc. A form, a colour exists only in relation to another. Form alone does not exist. We are only aware of relationships . . .' Such a concern for relationships seems to permeate Vuillard's numerous early still lifes. His *Still Life with Salad Bowl* (Plate 5) of 1887–8 was a more important and elaborate composition than most, one that may have belonged to the group of dining-room still lifes mentioned in the résumé in his journal, along with the *Still Life with Cabbage*, which had identical dimensions. (The former can be seen hanging in the dining-room of the rue Truffaut apartment in

3 *Mme Vuillard in the Dining-Room, rue Truffaut*. Dated 1900. Oil on cardboard, 15½ × 22¾ in. (39.5 × 57.7 cm.). Stuttgart, Staatsgalerie

4 Photograph by Vuillard. Dining-Room, rue Truffaut, *c.* 1899–1901, showing Vuillard's mother and sister, with Pierre Hermant and his wife Adrienne. Paris, Antoine Salomon

5 *Still Life with Salad Bowl. c.* 1887–8. Oil on canvas, 18⅛ × 25 in. (46 × 65 cm.). Paris, Musée d'Orsay

6 *Self-Portrait with Varoqui.* 1889. Oil on canvas, 36½ × 28½ in. (93 × 72.5 cm.). New York, The Metropolitan Museum of Art

Vuillard's photograph [Plate 4], and the latter in his interior of 1900 [Plate 3].) Against a tonal background, painted in short separate dabbed strokes, utensils and receptacles overlap with, intersect or reflect one another; a limited range of opalescent colours is used and carefully balanced so as to allow chords of unison to be struck. There is a studied casualness about the objects depicted: the pile of knives and plates, the uncut cheese, the bowl of salad as yet undressed await human use. Yet the whole arrangement has a balanced, symmetrical structure, reminiscent of Chardin.

Domestic still life was a useful means of exploring aesthetic principles hammered out with student friends and of trying out at home lessons learned in the Louvre in front of Chardin. Similarly, Vuillard's first experiments in portraiture were also made at home. In terms of scale and preparation, the *Self-Portrait with Varoqui* (Plate 6), painted in 1889, probably early in the year, represented his most ambitious undertaking to date. Perhaps it was intended as a Salon entry. In a sober, almost predominantly brown palette reminiscent of the tonal portraits of Whistler or Carrière, he tried out several newly learnt tricks of *trompe-l'oeil* illusionism; his status as an artist is indicated self-consciously, but discreetly, not through costume or setting but by the bottles of linseed oil or medium anchored in the foreground plane by nothing save their crisp, reflective surfaces, by the sheaf of brushes and by the palette he holds. But daringly, the palette is held at right angles to the spectator's gaze so that its characteristic shape is lost and it reads as no more than a single diagonal accent, glinting where its blobs of paint catch the light. A final, almost jokey touch is the small spot of red, isolating the smouldering tip of Varoqui's cigarette from the uniform brown tone of his beard. It is a tonal *tour de force*, in which Vuillard's proficiency as a still-life painter came to his aid.

The setting for this painting was Vuillard's grandmother's bedroom in the rue de Miromesnil apartment. Vuillard's maternal grandmother lived with the family until her death in 1893. Her bulky silhouette appears in several of his early interiors (*The Flowered Dress* for instance [Plate 10]), and she posed

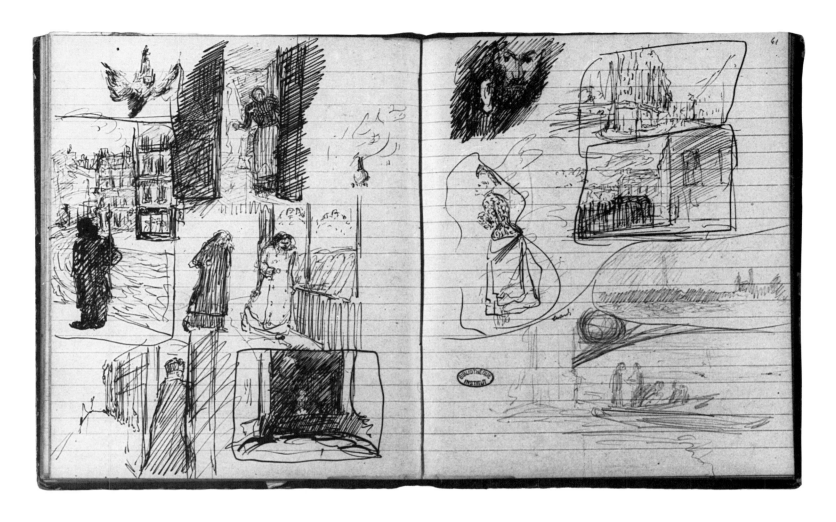

8 Sketches of Street Scenes and Figure Studies, from Vuillard's *Journal*, Carnet 1, Jan. 1890, pp. 40v and 41. Paris, Bibliothèque de l'Institut de France

7 *The Death of Caesar*. Compositional sketch, *c.* 1885. Pen and ink and wash on paper, 8 × 22⅜ in. (20.5 × 31.5 cm.). Private Collection

for the large, detailed and highly finished black chalk and charcoal drawing (Plate 11) which Vuillard submitted to the Salon jury in 1889. It was accepted.

The year 1889 was a satisfying one for Vuillard to see his first work shown at the Salon for it was the year of the Universal Exhibition, when Paris and the newly built Eiffel Tower were on show to the world. Not surprisingly, the Exhibition featured as a significant event in Vuillard's journal. But there is no mention of a certain notorious exhibition being unofficially staged in the Café Volpini in May and June by Paul Gauguin, Emile Bernard and their friends under the title 'Groupe Impressionniste et Synthétiste'. It makes one suspect that he had not yet received or responded to the message of Nabi synthetism first broadcast at the Académie Julian in 1888 by Paul Sérusier. Vuillard was still, in mid-1889, apparently more interested in the official exhibitions in the Palais des Beaux-Arts, where he could study the recent works of such prominent naturalists as Roll, Rixens and Besnard, as well as the earlier achievements of Corot and the Barbizon school, than in the revolutionary, crude, boldly coloured, primitive works of Gauguin and the Pont-Aven artists.

The so-called Nabis were a group of discontented students at the Académie Julian who had banded together in 1888–9 to form a secret brotherhood. Their leader, Sérusier, the student *massier* or monitor, had returned from his summer holiday in Brittany armed with a small embryonic landscape study made in Pont-Aven, directly under the instructions of Paul Gauguin. This little painting, *Landscape in the Bois d'Amour* (now in the Musée d'Orsay) seemed to hold the key to a new, simplified and synthetic way of working. Sérusier explained that by exaggerating the colours and simplifying the forms seen in nature, and by making use of memory, the artist could overcome the problem of being no more than a copyist. His first converts were his fellow students Maurice Denis, Pierre Bonnard, Paul Ranson and Henri-Gabriel Ibels, and they dubbed his landscape the 'Talisman'. United by their opposition to the unthinking naturalism that passed for art teaching at the time and committed to a higher, more ideal notion of art, they felt a calling as 'prophets' (Nabi means prophet in Hebrew) of the new synthetist discoveries of Gauguin.

The precise date at which Vuillard joined this group is difficult to pinpoint. We can safely describe him as a Nabi by 1890: in his journal he noted meeting both Bonnard and Sérusier in that year and later called 1890 'the Sérusier year'. His first contact within the group was Denis, whom he knew from the lycée Condorcet. Denis and Vuillard had more in common than might at first appear from their work. Both were enrolled at the Ecole des Beaux-Arts, both had strong religious backgrounds and philosophical leanings, both were fervent admirers of Puvis de Chavannes. They were certainly seeing each other in the summer of 1888 and in November that year, shortly after Sérusier's return from Brittany, Vuillard recorded meeting Denis at the home of another schoolfriend, Pierre Véber, later playwright and drama critic for *La Revue Blanche*. Yet if Denis tried to interest him on that occasion in the new ideas Sérusier was encouraging his followers to explore, Vuillard appears to have paid scant attention.

This apparent delay in Vuillard's coming to terms with the synthetist ideas of Sérusier may have a simple explanation. The large number of students enrolled at the Académie Julian meant that the teaching was organized around separate studios, each with its own *massier* and visiting professors. If Vuillard belonged to a different studio from the first Nabi recruits he would rarely have run into them, always supposing he kept up his attendance beyond 1887. A more important factor however, as will emerge later, would seem to have been Vuillard's innate resistance to the anti-naturalistic aesthetic his friends were advocating. It was not until some time in the late summer of 1889 that Denis was able to claim Vuillard as a valuable new addition to the Nabi cause, as is indicated by a letter he received from Sérusier, already in Brittany with Gauguin, written in the sonorous and archaic language typical of early Nabis correspondence: 'I envy you when you tell me about the new brother that Jahvé has directed towards us. Let him be welcome.'

9 *At the Ransons'. c.* 1895. Oil on cardboard, 19¼ × 22⅞ in. (49 × 58 cm.). Private Collection

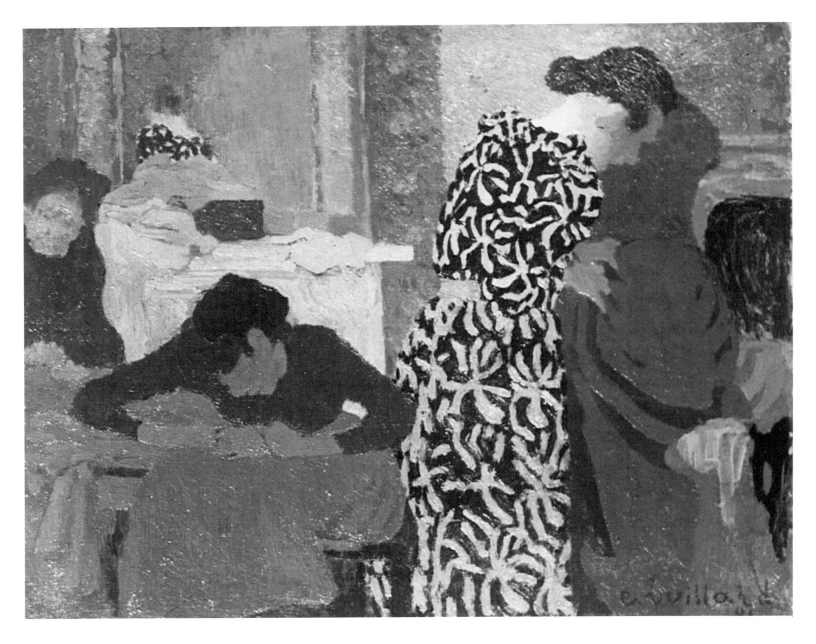

10 *The Flowered Dress.* Dated 1891. Oil on canvas, 14⅞ × 18 in. (37.7 × 45.5 cm.). Brazil, São Paulo Museum

11 *Portrait of Grandmother Michaud.* 1888–9. Conté crayon on paper, 16½ × 14⅛ in. (42 × 36 cm.). Private Collection

Chapter Two

VUILLARD AND THE NABIS

Denis's feeling of triumph at converting Vuillard to the Nabi cause was understandable, not only in view of the conviction and commitment of Vuillard to realism but also because of his evident talent and ambition, which both Denis and Sérusier were quick to acknowledge. In 1889 Vuillard had considerably more than most to lose in subjecting himself to the programme of re-education implied by his intellectual acceptance of the Nabis's ideas. Only that year he had, conventionally enough, put forward his candidature for the municipal competition to decorate the Salle des Mariages of the Mairie du XIVième. And that he was beset by misgivings is clear from numerous entries in his journal between 1890 and 1891. Inclined to be suspicious of theory and of its often remote application to practice, Vuillard nevertheless approached his work in a serious intellectual way and sought to rationalize his position in line with that of his friends.

One finds Vuillard trying to strike a balance between what he saw as the overly cerebral approach of Sérusier and the overly sensual, hedonistic attitudes of Roussel, who had followed Vuillard into the Nabi group. In so far as he concurred with Denis's rejection of the formulaic, banal recipes that had constituted their art teaching and shared his enthusiasm for the loftier achievements of a Puvis de Chavannes or a Fra Angelico, he felt duty bound to correct his own lazy, learned responses to the object, to stand back from nature and form of it a conceptualized 'idea' rather than reproducing, without forethought, what he saw. In early September 1890, for example, he noted:

Chardin's still lifes, the white and grey ones, (grapes, pipe) give pleasure through their tonal harmonies and their outline shapes and not by means of the greater or lesser degree of exactitude with which they recall their models which are unknown to us. The difficulty of establishing this firmly in my head after the long hours spent in front of those canvases two years ago imbued with naturalist ideas . . .

The message of the preeminence of formal means over subject-matter in conveying emotion in art had just been clearly spelt out in Denis's *Définition du Néo-Traditionnisme*, first published in the review *Art et Critique* in August 1890. 'Remember', instructed Denis, 'that a painting before it is a war horse, a nude woman or some anecdote, is first and foremost a flat surface covered with colours arranged in a certain order.' Under Denis's influence, Vuillard taught himself to be wary of the subject and to interrogate himself, even at times to admonish himself if he felt his literary interest in a motif was getting in the way of the purely pictorial concept. He almost seems to have taken its message to heart more fully than Denis himself; indeed, when interviewed in 1891 by the Symbolist critic Alphonse Germain for *La Plume*, Vuillard ventured to suggest that Denis would

12 *Sleep* or *Woman in Bed*. 1891–2.
Oil on canvas, 13 × 25¼ in.
(33 × 64 cm.). Paris, Musée d'Orsay
13 *Lugne-Poë*. Dated 1891. Oil on
cardboard laid on panel, 8¾ × 10½ in.
(22.2 × 26.5 cm.). New York,
Memorial Art Gallery of the
University of Rochester

14 *Pierre Bonnard painting*. 1891. Pencil on paper,
9½ × 5⅞ in. (24 × 14.5 cm.). Fontainebleau, Antoine
Terrasse

15 *Pierre Bonnard painting*. Inscribed and dated: 'à
Charles Bonnard Pierre Bonnard par E. Vuillard 91'.
Oil on board, 9⅞ × 5⅛ in. (24.6 × 12.8 cm.).
Fontainebleau, Antoine Terrasse

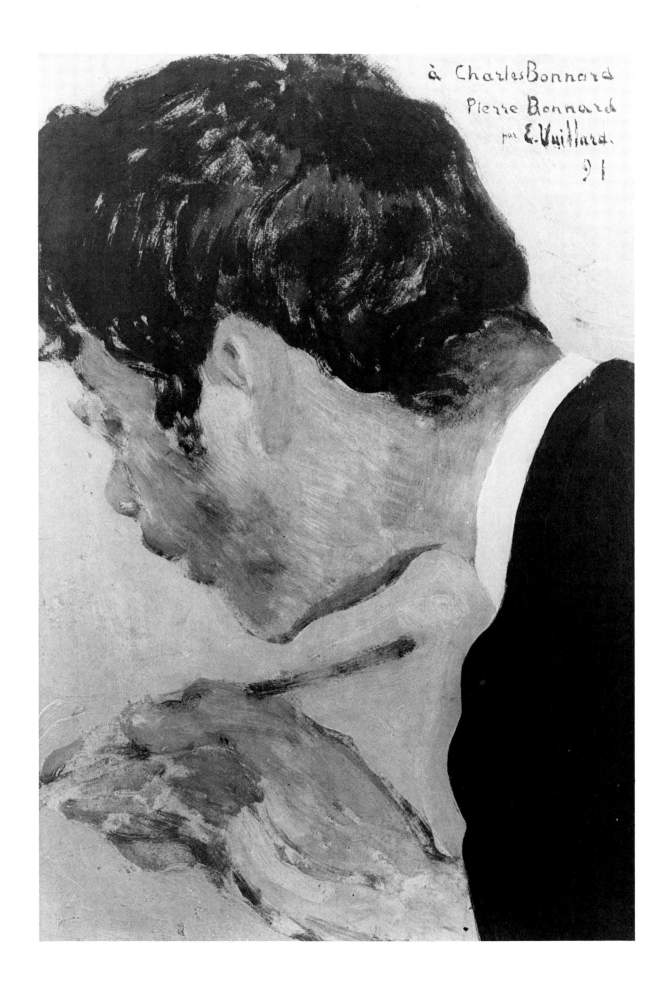

à Charles Bonnard
Pierre Bonnard
par E. Vuillard.
91

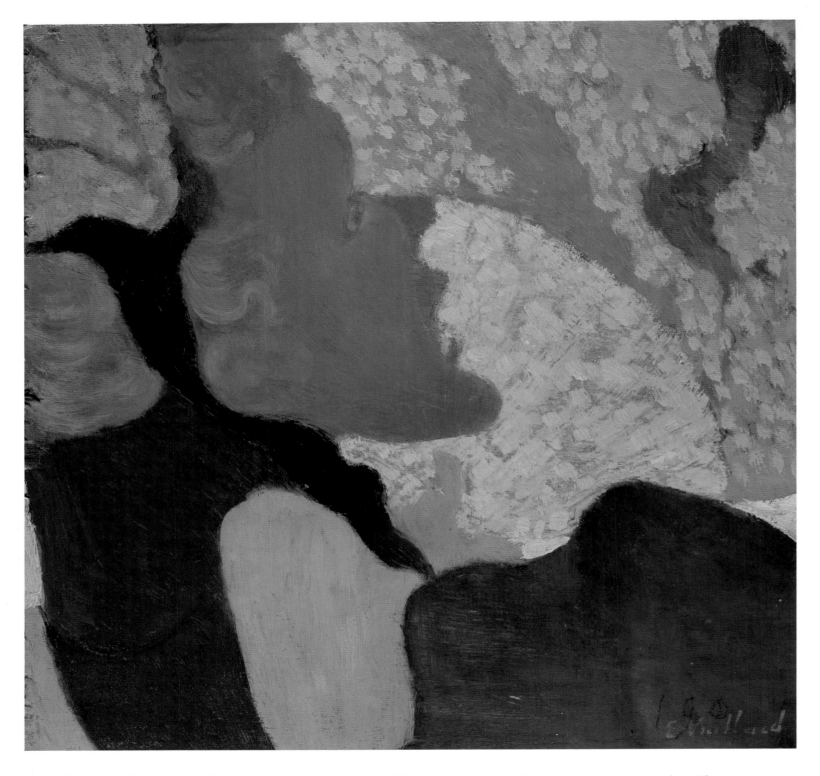

16 *Café-Concert Singer* or '*At The Divan Japonais*'. *c.* 1890–1. Oil on panel, 10⅝ × 10⅝ in. (27 × 27 cm.). London, Thomas Gibson Fine Art

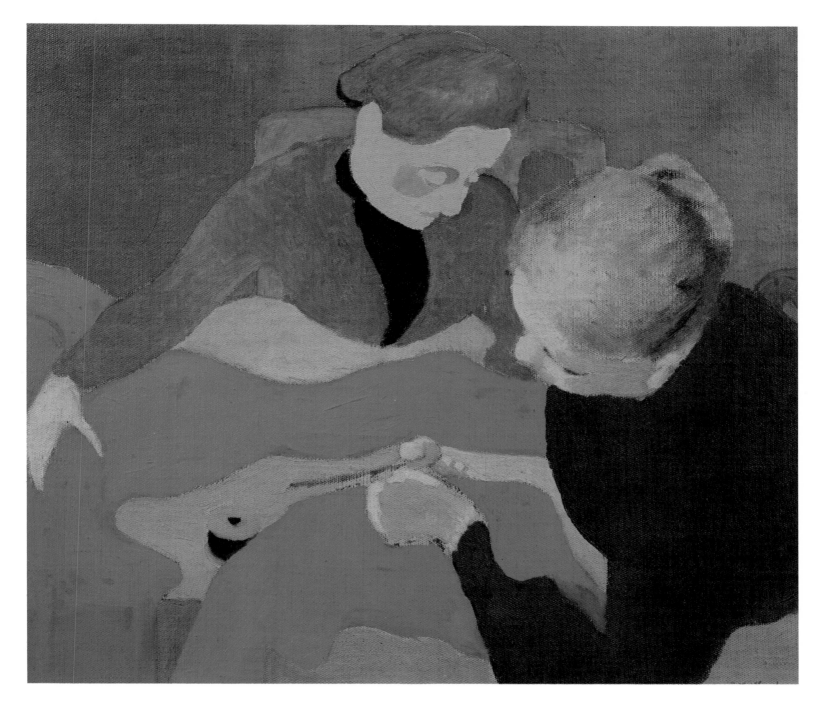

17 *Sewing. c.* 1890 (Design for a ceramic tile). Oil on canvas, 18⅞ × 22 in. (48 × 56 cm.). Josefowitz Collection

probably not have been so categorical in his arguments if he had been asked to reformulate the Definition.

By 1890 Vuillard had found a studio space for himself in the attic at the rue de Miromesnil. There he painted several self-portraits and made a large number of small studies, which Denis remarked upon when he visited him. Denis gave a positive bulletin on Vuillard's progress in a letter to Sérusier written some time in the early summer of 1890: 'Vuillard (whose newfound calm and joy so delights and astonishes him after his three years of feverishness and uncertainty) is producing, with great facility, the most delicate things one could imagine: always with an unexpected quality to their exquisite forms.' And in September Denis urged Vuillard to realize that he already had, in his sketchbooks, enough to keep him busy for years to come, material 'to develop, use and *turn into works of art*'. Vuillard himself noted that he had begun to work from memory late in 1889, turning out works that he deprecatingly referred to as 'petites salissures' – 'little daubs'.

Precisely because of their small size and experimental character, these 'petites salissures' are difficult to identify with any certainty. Like his friends, Vuillard took to painting on small panels or pieces of cardboard rather than on conventional canvas and to using a broader, flatter and more simplified application of paint occasionally raised with decorative textural dots. Although he did not entirely abandon his predilection for a low-key tonal palette (Plates 12, 13), around 1890–1 he began to try using arbitrary, brash colours, notably in works such as the *Café-Concert Singer* (Plate 16) of 1890 and in his theatre work of that year, the Théâtre Libre programme designs and the watercolours of Coquelin Cadet (Plate 139).

Like the other Nabis, Vuillard was trying in these small studies to achieve some sort of symbolic distillation of his experience. Shortly after a visit to a fair in September 1890, where he had been overwhelmed by the wealth of sensations, noises, voices, details, he sought to discover how he could convey them in paint. Paradoxically he seems to have been feeling his way towards a 'literary subject (in the decadent Verlaine sense)' as he termed it, a symbol to convey his emotion. His impression could not be rendered by the enumeration of the objects which determined it: 'a woman's head has just produced in me a certain emotion, I must make use of this emotion alone and I must not try to remember the nose or the ear, they're of no importance . . .' He went on to remind himself of the essential difference between a painting, which could never give more than an analogy of nature, and a snapshot. Vuillard's *Café-Concert Singer* can be seen as just such a distillation of the experience of a stage performance, the intense colour of the artificial lights, the heat and movement, the noise even. In a cooler tonality and more bucolic vein, *Man with Two Horses* (Plate 1), with its blocks of subdued colour and childlike drawing, typifies the seemingly artless simplicity of Vuillard's earliest Nabi works.

The role of drawing and particularly of silhouette in achieving this degree of almost caricatural simplification was crucial. Vuillard's sketches in 1890, frequently done in brush and Indian ink, were quick, quirky, animated silhouettes. They were closer to Japanese art and to the work of the 'Nabi très japonard', Pierre Bonnard, than to the heavy cloisonnist drawing style of Gauguin or Bernard which Vuillard only briefly essayed. Such exercises offered an alternative to the conventional use of modelled drawing as a preparation for painting. In his journal Vuillard contrasted the kind of tonal, chiaroscuro drawing he had been taught, whereby each stroke of the charcoal was accompanied by a smudge of the thumb to create the impression of roundness, with the pure silhouette which enabled one to see the form simply. Vuillard's caricatural drawings of actors, some of which were used in the design for the *The Drama Competition* (Plate 22), almost certainly date from this period. They will be discussed more fully, in the context of Vuillard's own involvement with the theatre, in Chapter Four. At times, as in his drawn and painted portraits of Bonnard (Plates 14, 15), one can see Vuillard introducing a systematic reductionism, not easily or instinctively but with the same deliberation and balancing he had practised in his still lifes.

In 1891, when his family moved from the rue de Miromesnil to the rue Saint-Honoré, Vuillard began to

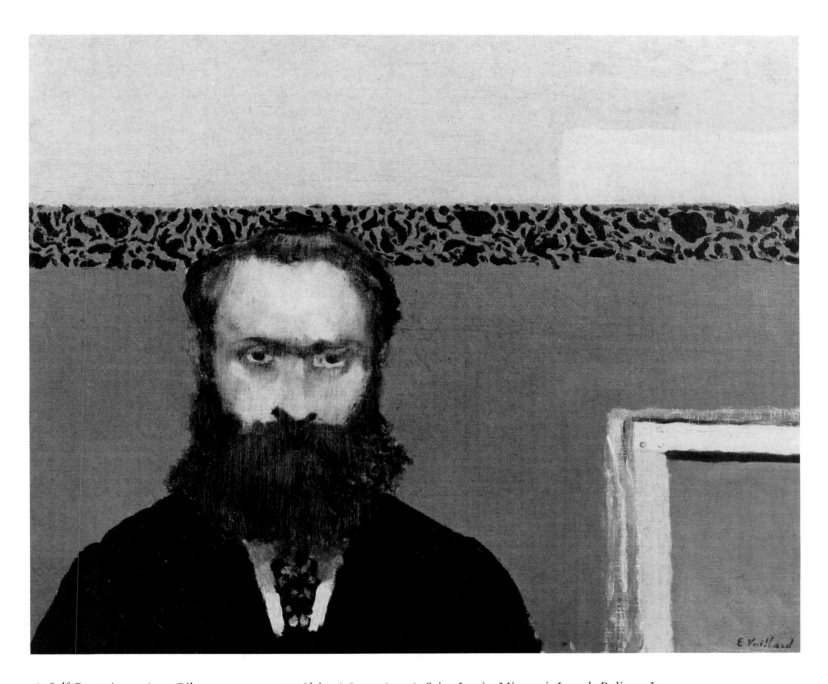

18 *Self-Portrait. c.* 1892. Oil on canvas, 15 × 18¼ in. (38 × 46 cm.). Saint Louis, Missouri, Joseph Pulitzer Jr.

19 *Seated Nude*. 1890–1. Oil on cardboard, 11 × 8 in. (28.5 × 21 cm.). Josefowitz Collection

20 *Self-Portrait. c.* 1890. Oil on octagonal cardboard, 14¼ × 11 in. (36 × 28 cm.). Private Collection

work with his new friends Bonnard, Denis and the young actor Lugné-Poe in a cramped studio at 28 rue Pigalle, near the artists' quarter. By this time he was already considered by Denis as the member of the group most likely to succeed. Already, thanks to Lugné's intervention, he had been involved with programme design for the Théâtre Libre and the actor Coquelin Cadet was interested in his drawings. It was probably during this stimulating period of working in each others' pockets that Vuillard painted his friends' portraits, and his startlingly synthetic *Self-Portraits* (Plates 18, 20). He shared the expense of hiring models with Bonnard and both painted the same nude from different angles in 1891 (Plate 19). However, Vuillard was an artist who preferred and needed solitude. Although the friendships and exchanges of ideas were cherished and he would continue to participate in Nabi group ventures such as theatre design and puppet plays, by the end of 1891 he had rented a separate studio two doors away.

It has often been said that Vuillard was reluctant to exhibit his work. Certainly he seems to have made no effort to submit work to the Salon des Indépendants as Bonnard and Denis did, with marked success, from 1891 onwards. Nor did he make a very forceful presence in the Nabis's first group exhibitions at the Château de Saint-Germain-en-Laye in the summer of 1891 and at Le Barc de Boutteville's gallery later that year. But the picture that has been built up of Vuillard's reticence is only partly correct. If in the early 1890s his name featured less frequently than his contemporaries' as an exhibitor, he was, nevertheless, already being courted by buyers and written about by critics. He seems to have had his first modest showing of work at the offices of *La Revue Blanche* in the rue des Martyrs in 1892, and he showed a group of small studies, mostly of interiors, at Le Barc de Boutteville's gallery in November that year which were judged by Rémy de Gourmont and other critics to be divertingly varied and of 'evident interest'. In 1893 he exhibited at least thirteen works on different occasions and the following year joined in an important Nabi group exhibition organized by the enterprising newspaper editor Arthur Huc at the premises of *La Dépêche* in Toulouse. Thereafter his works were widely shown, both in public exhibitions and at dealers' galleries.

As well as launching themselves in the eyes of the public through group exhibitions, the Nabis were also trying out different media in the 1890s. Vuillard's extraordinarily schematic painting *Sewing* (Plate 17), painted around 1892, was apparently related to a project to design a ceramic tile, which may explain its almost square format. Although the tile seems not to have materialized, the painting's stark simplicity, pleasing arabesques and bold colour contrasts suggest it would have worked well in that medium. In 1895 Samuel Bing gave Vuillard, among others, a chance to venture into stained-glass design (Plate 23). These designs were exhibited, along with a decorated dinner service, at Bing's Salon de l'Art Nouveau that same year. The widespread revival of interest in the graphic arts in the 1890s did not escape Vuillard's attention; he tried his hand at printmaking, ventured into advertising with his *Bécane* poster (Plate 21) and made some remarkably accomplished and subtle coloured lithographs. Throughout 1893 *La Revue Blanche* offered its readers a monthly artist's print, most of them designed by Nabis, and in 1897 Vuillard was commissioned to produce a lithographic series, *Landscapes and Interiors*, by the dealer Ambroise Vollard, a series in which he built on the subject-matter and decorative use of pattern and colour already explored in his painting (Plates 29, 30).

By the time of his first exhibition at Vollard's gallery at the beginning of 1897 (Vollard took up the Nabis around 1896 following Le Barc's sudden death), Vuillard's name was firmly associated in critics' minds with small, often disconcertingly mysterious interiors. Apart from Thadée Natanson, whose reviews frequently hinted at the greater breadth of which he knew Vuillard was capable and who discerned and applauded a more 'general' approach in Vuillard's interiors after 1898, most critics were ignorant of Vuillard's work as a decorator. Even a fellow exhibitor at Le Barc's gallery, Paul Signac, had to confess his astonishment when Vuillard first took him to see some of the panels that he had painted for private apartments.

21 *Bécane* (Poster for a meat extract drink). *c.* 1894. Colour lithograph, 32¼ × 24 in. (81.5 × 61 cm.). Paris, Bibliothèque Nationale

22 *The Drama Competition of the Academy.* 1890. Brush and Indian ink and watercolour on paper, 13⅜ × 11⅜ in. (34 × 29 cm.). London, Victoria and Albert Museum, Theatre Museum

23 *The Chestnut Trees*. Study for a stained-glass window for Samuel Bing. 1895.
Distemper on canvas, 43¼ × 27½ in. (110 × 70 cm.). Josefowitz Collection

Since entries in the journal are infrequent between 1894 and 1907, the series of important and datable decorative commissions Vuillard undertook in the 1890s and early 1900s provides fixed points which help us to chart his changes of style and subject-matter during these years. Most of the commissions came from members of the Natanson family and their circle. Alexandre and Thadée Natanson, wealthy sons of a Polish-Jewish banker, were the co-funders and editors of *La Revue Blanche*, whose editorial office moved from Belgium to Paris in 1891. Vuillard's first commission was to paint six panels for the 'chic bourgeois salon' (as his fellow Nabi Paul Ranson put it), in fact the study-cum-cabinet de toilette, of Paul Desmarais, a cousin by marriage of the Natansons. Vuillard chose themes from modern life and divided the modest, emphatically horizontal panels into three sets of pairs: figures in a public garden, dressmakers in their workshop and figures on a terrace (Plates 25, 26, 27). While the outdoor scenes are characterized by a feeling of space akin to the spare rhythms of a Fra Angelico predella, the seamstresses' workshop is more Japanese, conjoining Vuillard's interest in silhouette – slender, corseted women caught in the act of turning, leaning, stooping or stretching – with his eye for pattern and colour: flowers, stripes and checks vie with one another to animate the flattened space. The project kept Vuillard busy throughout the summer of 1892 and was discussed and admired, although Vuillard never exhibited the panels. Roger Marx, a great champion of the applied arts, drew attention to Vuillard's fresh and original response to the demands of decoration in *Le Voltaire*, and predicted a promising future for the Nabis as decorators, in view of the sensitivity to the 'rhythm of a line, the quality of an arabesque, the alternations of calm and movement, void and solid'.

For two of the Desmarais panels, as for so many of his small interiors of this date (Plates 17, 49), his mother's rue Saint-Honoré workshop provided Vuillard with a ready-made motif. The seamstress was a popular realist image, as Vuillard must have been aware, often used to carry moralizing connotations. His seamstresses, who included his sister Marie, are depicted as absorbed by their tasks, young and graceful but not conventionally coquettish. In refusing them all depth, in line with Nabi principles and Japanese precedents, he avoided any suggestion of moral or literary overtones. Vuillard pursued the seamstress theme in a five-panelled screen (Plate 24), commissioned by Paul Desmarais in 1892 to accompany the overdoors. Although the setting was the same, Vuillard made a more ambiguous use of space in these asymmetrical panels, contrasting flattening verticals with an illusionistic perspectival floor plan. He began work on the screen shortly after returning from a brief visit to Belgium, Holland and London with Roussel, and the admiration he had felt before the so-called primitives, particularly the Angelicos and Lippis, in the National Gallery perhaps accounts for this new polyptych-like use of space. The excursion had also, somewhat perversely in view of Nabi predilections for flat, primitive art, revived his enthusiasm for the realism of the seventeenth-century Dutch genre painters.

The reason for this sudden, unplanned pilgrimage to northern art galleries was the need to extricate his friend Roussel from an unfortunate entanglement with a certain Caro. Roussel's turbulent affairs of the heart were always of immediate concern for Vuillard, particularly after they became brothers-in-law in July 1893 when Roussel married Vuillard's sister Marie. Coincidentally, two of Vuillard's other close friends married this same year, Denis and Thadée Natanson, leaving him feeling 'terribly celibate' as he confided with some pain in a letter to the Dutch Nabi Jan Verkade. Verkade was one of the Nabis who opted for a totally celibate life, along with the Dane Mogens Ballin, when both converted to Catholicism and joined an order of Benedictine monks in Germany. Vuillard was not tempted thus far into celibacy. He cryptically mentions 'histoires sentimentales' in his journal for 1894 and was evidently susceptible to the attractions of the opposite sex. Thadée Natanson's young wife, the talented and kittenish Polish pianist Misia Godebska, made a profound impact on him. The Natansons were immensely hospitable, both in their small Paris apartment in

24 *The Desmarais Screen – Seamstresses.* 1892. Photograph showing the five vertical panels and five upper panels in original frame. Paris, Antoine Salomon. The upper panels and frame are lost; the five vertical panels dispersed

25, 26, 27 *Stroking the Dog*, *Gardening* and *The Dressmaker's Workshop I*. 1892. Three of the six Desmarais panels. Oil on canvas, 19⅛ × 46⅛ in. (48.5 × 117 cm.). Private Collection

the rue Saint-Florentin, which appears in various of Vuillard's interiors (Frontispiece, Plate 50), and at their country homes, first at Valvins, near Fontainebleau, and then a little further south at Villeneuve-sur-Yonne (Plates 35, 36). Their lively social circle drew in not only Vuillard and Bonnard but also Toulouse-Lautrec and the Swiss painter Félix Vallotton, who joined the Nabis in 1892, quite apart from the many journalists, poets and playwrights associated with *La Revue Blanche*.

Following the success of the Desmarais panels, the eldest and most wealthy of the Natanson brothers, Alexandre, commissioned Vuillard to paint a series of nine large panels for the dining-room of his smart new town house. Built for his wife by his parents-in-law, 60 avenue du Bois was situated on the main leafy thoroughfare leading to the Bois de Boulogne, one of the most fashionable addresses in Paris at the end of the last century. One can follow Vuillard's search for an appropriate subject in his journal during the summer months of 1894. His decision to develop the modern-life theme of the *Public Gardens* (Plates 32, 33) can be seen as a response to Impressionism. But unlike Seurat, whose *Sunday Afternoon on the Ile de la Grande-Jatte* was an obvious precedent, or Degas, whose habit of specializing in similar 'types' of women – maids, dancers, prostitutes – had been a subject for discussion with Bonnard that year, Vuillard would make no attempt to turn the inhabitants of his parks into stock urban types or to make any overt comment on them. It was Monet's garden paintings that he evoked, particularly in his treatment of light and coloured shadow.

The most prominent figures in Vuillard's *Public Gardens* are the nursemaids. In his journal he noted and sketched with a naturalist's eye for detail the appearance of one nursemaid, who had sat herself down on the bench next to him for two days running: 'dress with little squares, creases that have no suppleness, like paper, black bodice old creases with no roundness to them, white apron. The quality of the creases small and stiff, hair like wet seaweed, stiff, matt complexion, mouth purplish blue today; the kid wan-looking, distressed by the weather, silky hair, crisp white clothes.' He also made pen and ink sketches of clumps of regularly spaced trees, of patterns of shadow and of children playing, which laid the foundations for his large panels (Plate 31); and he fixed the compositions in a series of small pastels which helped him to envisage the colour and decorative schema as a whole. But as Vuillard's ideas for the decorations (or 'tapisseries' as he called them) became more focused, he urged himself to concentrate on the pictorial values that had initially inspired him – the contrast between the light transparent foliage and the dense opaque material of the clothes, for instance – and to avoid making the drawing or location too specific: 'Really for a decoration for an apartment a subject that's objectively too precise could easily become unbearable. One would grow less quickly tired of a textile, of designs that don't have too much literary precision.' Thus no specific park is depicted, rather we are offered an amalgam of Vuillard's impressions of the Tuileries, the Square de la Trinité and the Bois de Boulogne itself. The vertical panels interrelate space and figure in much the same way as those in Puvis's first Sainte-Geneviève cycle in the Panthéon. And the supple liveliness of Vuillard's figures, which so belie those first disdainful observations in his journal, remind one that at this time he was also making regular visits to the Louvre, where his attention seems to have been especially drawn by Watteau (Plate 34). Such an interest may in part account for the psychological delicacy with which he depicted the exchange between the boys in *The Two Schoolboys* (Plate 33) and that between the woman and child in *Asking Questions* (Plate 32).

In the five panels of *Women and Flowers* commissioned by Thadée Natanson in 1895, one of which can be seen hanging on the wall in his later painting of *Vallotton and Misia in the Dining-Room, rue Saint-Florentin* (Frontispiece), the treatment of space was far more soft and dense, still more tapestry-like; but in the *Figures and Interiors* (Plates 42, 43), a series of four panels commissioned in 1896 by the successful young doctor Henri Vaquez, later Proust's physician, Vuillard deployed a stricter grid of verticals and horizontals to offset the potentially claustrophobic riot of pattern. In this case, for all that the subject was ostensibly a modern

28 *Woman Seated in a Bar. c.* 1893–5. Distemper and gouache on paper, $8\frac{1}{4} \times 5\frac{1}{2}$ in. (20.3 × 13.9 cm.). Paris, Musée d'Orsay (Louvre, Cabinet des Dessins)

29 *The Pastry Shop*. 1897–8. Colour lithograph from the series *Landscapes and Interiors*, publ. Vollard, 1899.
13⅞ × 10⅝ in. (35.5 × 27 cm.). London, British Museum

30 *Interior with Pink Wallpaper, II.* 1897–8. Colour lithograph from the series *Landscapes and Interiors*, publ. Vollard, 1899. 13¾ × 11 in. (35 × 28 cm.). London, British Museum

interior, the panels were unquestionably inspired by the *mille fleurs* tapestries Vuillard had admired in the Musée de Cluny (Plate 40). He even gave his colour range the look of tapestry, choosing pinks, greens and ochres. Upon completion in 1897 the four panels were installed in Vaquez's library. They can be seen today as an intact decorative scheme in the Musée du Petit Palais in Paris.

The medium Vuillard had used for these large series of panels was *peinture à la colle* or distemper. He had first used *colle* as a scene-painter in the theatre and liked its quick-drying properties as well as its chalky, unreflective surface, which harmonized well in an interior setting. He would continue to use *colle* in preference to any other paint medium throughout his career, both for decorative and for easel painting, believing it less liable to discolour with age than varnished oil paint; however, in some of his works, problems of cracking have occurred, especially where he seems to have built up the paint surface without allowing sufficient time for each layer to dry. In cultivating a dry, matt quality, Vuillard was in tune with most of the decorative painters of his generation who, in the wake of Puvis and Gauguin, sought to avoid the illusion of depth and reflective properties associated with oil paint and to approximate, in different ways, the flat wall-enhancing effects of fresco.

Although not a commissioned decoration, the scale and composite interior theme of the *Large Interior with Six Figures* (Plate 68) relate it to the Vaquez panels and it may have been painted with the Natansons' country home at Valvins in mind. Vuillard seems to have given the painting, possibly as part of an exchange, to his friend Vallotton, perhaps recognizing that he had come close here to the kind of bourgeois interiors in which Vallotton himself specialized, interiors in which the unspoken tensions between the figures invite psychological analysis. However, as ever, Vuillard avoided any clear narrative reading by leaving the interrelationships between the various figures ambiguous. A number of them can be tentatively identified: Mme Vuillard, seated to the left, appears to be talking to Marie, Vuillard's sister, while the figure leaning into the picture space on the right could be Misia Natanson. The claustrophobic atmosphere produced by the dominant reds and the ambiguous play of flatness and depth evoke a mood that has been described, with justification, as Mallarméan. The features of the man at the desk could almost be those of the poet; Mallarmé was a close friend and neighbour of the Natansons at Valvins, and a great admirer of Vuillard's work. Bonnard remarked to Vuillard at about this time how much one of his drawings reminded him of Mallarmé's poetry, both being difficult to decipher at first (as in Plate 30). And in 1898 Mallarmé was very keen that Vuillard should illustrate his recently completed poem *Hérodiade*. Sadly his death in September that year prevented what would have been a fascinating collaboration between painter and poet.

Vuillard can be associated with other writers who were broadly representative of the Symbolist aesthetic in the 1890s. Marcel Proust, an occasional contributor to *La Revue Blanche*, was exploring the literary value of repeated sensation and remembered experience, while the playwright Maurice Maeterlinck was proclaiming the artistic value of those quiet moments in life when nothing much happens outwardly and everything happens inwardly. Vuillard too found artistic resonance in the commonplace scene or familiar repeated gesture. Like Mallarmé, he could conjure up the levels of unforeseen mystery lying at the heart of the most mundane, domestic observations. In his journal for 1893 he asked himself: 'Why is it in the familiar places that the mind and the sensibility find the greatest degree of genuine novelty?'

The two large decorative panels Vuillard was commissioned to paint for Jean Schopfer in 1898, *Figures in the Garden of Le Relais, Villeneuve-sur-Yonne* (Plates 35, 36), both represent the garden of Le Relais, the former posthouse of Villeneuve-sur-Yonne, where Thadée and Misia Natanson had their new country residence. Several of the figures are clearly identifiable. Misia is depicted in the right-hand panel, lounging on a garden chair; in the other panel Marthe de Meligny is shown browsing through an illustrated fashion

31 Page of compositional sketches and notes relating to the *Public Gardens* decorations, from Vuillard's *Journal*, Carnet 2, July 1894, p. 49. Paris, Bibliothèque de l'Institut de France

32 Overleaf (left) *Little Girls Playing* and (right) *Asking Questions*. Two of the nine panels of *Public Gardens* for Alexandre Natanson. Dated 1894. Distemper on canvas, 84¾ × 34¾ in. (214.5 × 88 cm.); 84¾ × 37¼ in. (214.5 × 94 cm.). Paris, Musée d'Orsay

33 Overleaf (right) *The Two Schoolboys*. One of the nine panels of *Public Gardens*. Dated 1894. Distemper on canvas, 83½ × 37¾ in. (212 × 96 cm.). Brussels, Musées Royaux des Beaux-Arts

34 Jean-Antoine Watteau: *Gathering in a Park*. 1717. Oil on canvas, 12½ × 18 in. (32 × 46 cm.). Paris, Musée du Louvre (La Caze Collection)

magazine, her companion Pierre Bonnard, seen from behind, playing with a kitten. The other guests amuse themselves in the surrounding garden while a domestic servant discreetly provides for their needs. With their understated colour range of soft greens and greys, enlivened with carmine, these decorations carry echoes of earlier images of the leisured bourgeoisie at play, of eighteenth-century *fêtes champêtres*. Yet they are also very much images of their time. In the 1890s *villégiatures*, those lengthy summer holidays and expansive house parties in the country, were a bourgeois privilege. With the advent of the railway, provincial towns such as Villeneuve-sur-Yonne were now readily accessible from Paris; guests could turn up for the day or the weekend, or, if they were like Vuillard, stay for months on end. Vuillard was later to look back on these convivial gatherings and their idyllic setting as some of the happiest times of his life. Thadée Natanson, whose marriage to Misia was destined to be short-lived, also wrote fondly of these summers when Toulouse-Lautrec played court jester – swimming in the Yonne, marching through a storm, donning fancy costume, and generally shocking the other guests.

Jean Schopfer, who later wrote novels under the pen-name of Claude Anet, perhaps commissioned these decorations as an act of faith in Vuillard. In a series of articles on French art published in *La Revue Blanche*, he had blamed the influence of the academic system, its slavish obedience to Rome and its woeful neglect of France's native artistic tradition for the impoverished state of the decorative arts in his own era. He had already commissioned Vuillard to decorate a service of dinner plates in 1895, for which Vuillard used the motif of heads of young Parisiennes, rather in the manner of Toulouse-Lautrec, and he would go on to commission a third large panel to complete the decorative scheme begun in 1898 (Plate 41). This was subsequently altered and split into the two panels which now hang in the National Gallery in London.

In 1899 Vuillard painted two monumental landscape decorations, *Landscapes – Ile de France* (Plates 37, 38). This time the commission was from Adam Natanson, the father of Thadée and Alexandre, no doubt at his sons' urging. All Vuillard's 1890s decorative work distantly recalls Puvis de Chavannes but here, perhaps in deference to his client's taste, which was almost certainly more conservative than that of his sons, Vuillard seems consciously to have turned back to his great mentor. Puvis was much written about in the wake of his death in 1898, his methods of working and his ideas on the use of memory in painting were often discussed, as was his place in the context of Symbolism. Robert de la Sizeranne, in his obituary of Puvis, isolated the landscape as the element of Puvis's murals which lent them their poetry: 'One can well imagine the *Sacred Grove* without its Muses, *Winter* without its woodcutters. They would remain magnificent pages and their poetry would scarcely be diminished. It's the landscape which assures the figures their harmony and unity.' Vuillard's panels seem to demonstrate de la Sizeranne's point. Inspired by the landscapes around L'Etang-la-Ville where Ker and Marie Roussel had recently settled, he concentrated on the masses of foliage, the harmonious rhythms of forest, ridge and sky and gave only a marginal place to figures. The general composition, the broad horizontal format, the painted floral borders, the consciously muted palette of greys and grey-greens are all reminiscent of Puvis (Plate 39). Achille Segard, whose two-volume study *Les Décorateurs* provides an invaluable catalogue of Vuillard's decorative commissions up to 1914, found the merit of these panels was that 'they keep quiet if they are not being spoken to yet they discreetly accompany the thoughts of the visitor if he addresses himself to them.' These, together with the Villeneuve and Vaquez panels, represent some of Vuillard's highest achievements in the realm of mural decoration.

35, 36 *Figures in the Garden of Le Relais, Villeneuve-sur-Yonne*. Dated 1898. Two panels for Jean Schopfer. Distemper on canvas, 84½ × 63½ in. (213.7 × 160.9 cm.). Private Collection

37, 38 *Window looking on to the Woods, l'Etang-la-Ville* and *First Fruits* (detail). Dated 1899. Two panels (*Landscapes – Ile de France*) for Adam Natanson. Oil on canvas. The former, 98 × 149 in. (249.2 × 378.5 cm.), Art Institute of Chicago; the latter, 97 × 157 in. (248 × 400 cm.), Pasadena, California, Norton Simon Foundation

39 Pierre Puvis de Chavannes: *The Sacred Grove beloved of the Arts and the Muses* (detail showing decorative border). 1884.
Oil on canvas, 181⅛ × 409½ in. (460 × 1040 cm.). Lyons, Musée des Beaux-Arts

40 *'The Lady with the Unicorn'. Taste.* Late 15th century. One of a series of six tapestries. 148 × 181 in. (376 × 460 cm.). Paris, Musée de Cluny

41 Photograph by Vuillard showing *Lunch in the Garden at La Terrasse, Vasouy* in situ and as one panel, as it was painted for Jean Schopfer in 1901. Paris, Antoine Salomon. Reworked later (in 1935) into two panels. Distemper on canvas, existing panels measure 86 × 75 in. (218 × 190 cm.) and 86 × 72 in. (218 × 182 cm.). London, National Gallery

42, 43 *Music* and *The Work Table*. Dated 1896.
Two of the four panels of *Figures and Interiors* for
Dr Vaquez. Distemper on canvas, 83½ × 60⅝ in. (212
× 154 cm.) and 83½ × 29 in. (212 × 75 cm.). Ville
de Paris, Musée du Petit Palais, Paris

Chapter Three

INDEPENDENT STATUS AND CRITICAL SUCCESS

The Nabi group dissolved, without any traumatic break, as the 1890s drew to a close. Although the Nabi artists remained friends and would continue to exhibit together when occasion arose, by the turn of the century the stronger talents among them had achieved an independent status and no longer identified so closely with the aims of the original group.

A measure of the Nabis's success over the preceding decade was the fact that in March 1899 they staged their important and, in the event, final group exhibition at the prestigious Durand-Ruel gallery. They were shown alongside the Neo-Impressionists and a few independent figures, the most significant of whom was Odilon Redon. The Paris correspondent of *The Studio*, Gabriel Mourey, singled out Vuillard as the only artist in the exhibition worthy of attention: 'his "scènes d'intérieur" are truly exquisite and full of sensitive delicacy and harmonious expression of the most personal kind.' In *La Revue Blanche* Thadée Natanson described Vuillard's and Bonnard's work as peerless. Vuillard's magical way with colour, creating impressions of richness and splendour from materials and objects of the humblest origins, brought Watteau and Chardin to mind; his subordination of figures and movements to an overall coloured confusion of objects was likened to the way the heavy orchestration of the day absorbed the sound of the human voice. (Unfortunately the generic title 'scènes d'intérieur' was used for the four Vuillard paintings listed in the catalogue, making it difficult to know exactly which pictures these critics were talking about, although they certainly included Plate 52.) Commenting on the exhibition, Denis judged the Nabis to have separated into two distinct factions. Whereas he, Sérusier and Ranson showed a preference for working on the grand public scale in pure colours, with symbolic forms and 'certain documents' elaborated in advance in the studio, the other main group, consisting of Vuillard, Bonnard and Vallotton, preferred to work on a scale that was adapted to private apartments, relied more closely on nature, filtered through memory, and used sombre colouring and complex handling.

Although, as we have seen, Vuillard was by this date quite up to tackling large-scale work and often used a light-toned palette, Denis's general characterization of his working methods remains valid. He and Vuillard had a free and frank exchange of views in their correspondence early in 1898, following a short period spent together in Florence, which threw into relief growing differences in their approach to their work. Denis, influenced by his recent study of Ingres, Poussin and Raphael, was increasingly preoccupied by the necessity, for him, of establishing a disciplined method and a clearly worked-out stylistic theory, whereas Vuillard confessed to having an aversion for general ideas on art which he had not arrived at for himself; his abhorrence of theory led him, somewhat apologetically, to rely on sensation and instinct. His working practice consisted of flashes of enthusiastic confidence interspersed with hesitant, uninspired periods. For Denis, Vuillard's

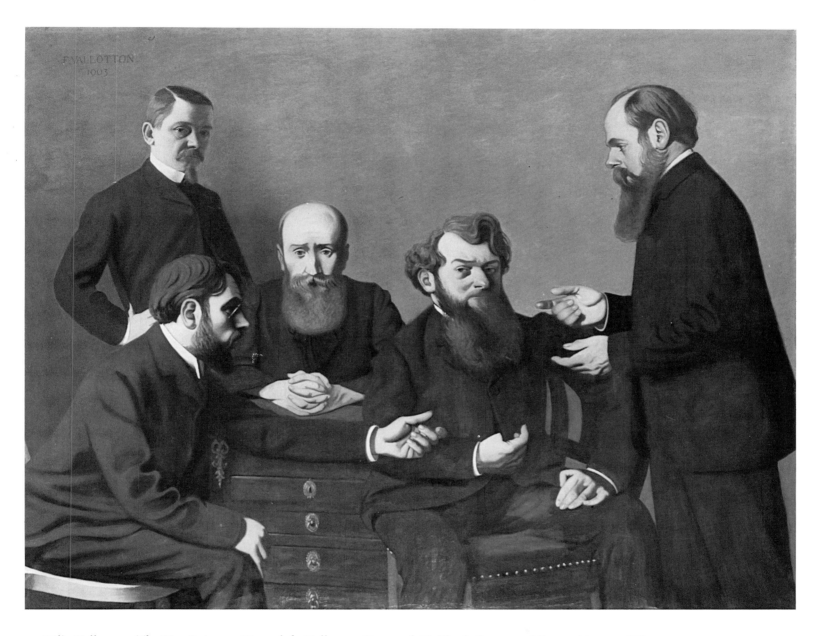

44 Félix Vallotton: *The Five Painters*. (From left, Vallotton, Bonnard, Vuillard, Cottet and Roussel.) 1903. Oil on canvas, 57 × 73⅞ in. (145 × 187.5 cm.). Winterthur, Kunstmuseum

45 *Cargo Boat at the Quayside, Hamburg.* 1913. Distemper on paper, 21 × 20⅝ in. (53 × 52 cm.). Paris, Musée d'Orsay

46 *Window on Lac Léman.* Dated 1900. Oil on cardboard, 24⅜ × 19¼ in. (62 × 49 cm.). Zurich, Feilchenfeldt

47 *Odilon Redon at Saint Georges de Didonne*. 1901. Pen and
ink on paper, $5\frac{1}{4} \times 4$ in. (13.4 × 9.9 cm.). Private Collection

sensual, instinctive approach bore witness to his 'superabundance' of natural talent. It put him on a par with
the Impressionists, and was thus essentially at odds with the original Nabi ideals, with their admiration for the
great hieratic decorative tradition of the past. Indeed, according to the first-hand account of Segard, it was at
about this time that Vuillard recalled having been amazed by major showings of the work of Degas and Monet.

The very real artistic and temperamental differences between Denis and Vuillard were compounded by
the opposing stands they adopted on that pressing social and political issue of the day, the Dreyfus affair.
Denis, as a right-wing Catholic, joined the anti-Dreyfusard faction and signed the anti-Semitic petition of
Edmond Drumont in *La Libre Parole*; Vuillard, being closely involved with *La Revue Blanche*, most of whose
contributors were Jewish, was a committed Dreyfusard and early in 1899 signed the opposing petition in
Clemenceau's radical newspaper *L'Aurore*, which condemned the judgement against Dreyfus and called for a
retrial. It was a rare case of Vuillard taking a political stand and he clearly found the divisive issue exceedingly
painful. Thadée Natanson recalled that when the results of the retrial became known in September 1899
(Dreyfus was again found guilty but with extenuating circumstances) Vuillard broke down in tears, not out of
sympathy with Dreyfus, he explained, but out of grief for his country.

In this situation, Vuillard found himself aligned with the Neo-Impressionist artists whose radicalism
had never been in doubt – Paul Signac and Maximilien Luce – although he does not seem to have gone as far as
his friend Roussel in espousing anarchist views. When visiting Vuillard's studio in 1898, Signac was disposed
to find favour but was struck by the contrast between his own work and Vuillard's. He compared the Neo-
Impressionists' attempt to apply a controlled method and synthetic approach to reality with what he saw as
Vuillard's liberation from reality, his tendency to fantasize and to latch on to the charm of a chance but
unformed observation. 'We are too precise, he not precise enough,' he concluded. Set against Vuillard's
spontaneous, painterly approach, his exquisite colour sense and his wilful negligence of detail, Signac found

48 Photograph by Vuillard. Misia Natanson in her salon, rue Saint-Florentin. *c.* 1898. Paris, Antoine Salomon

his own work too photographic, too closely based on nature. And in 1901, assessing the talents Denis demonstrated in his religious decorations at the chapel of Le Vésinet, Vuillard noted how his friend excelled at giving a solid support to fragile charm, a precision of forms to imprecise sentiments. Vuillard could not share Denis's love of classicism, which was increasingly visible in the clarity of his forms and the frieze-like symmetry of his compositions. Nor could he see how Denis's new hero Cézanne could be understood in classical terms, reasonably enough pointing out Cézanne's kinship with Veronese, and thus with the baroque colourist tradition; and he had only half-heartedly espoused the Nabis's fervent admiration for Gauguin, whom he considered something of a 'pedant'.

This polarization in the ideas of Vuillard and Denis, in a sense between genre painting and classicism, prefigured a crucial debate in the development of French painting between the turn of the century and the First World War and even beyond. Both Maurice Denis and Paul Signac were artists whose aesthetic ideas proved to have a strong influence on the new generation; the return to classical values manifested itself in the work of artists as diverse as Cross, Maillol, Roussel (Plate 88), and, significantly, the rising stars of Fauvism, Matisse and Derain, all of whom experimented with idyllic, arcadian themes and felt the timeless lure of the Mediterranean as the cradle of ancient civilization. One might argue that the careers of Matisse, Bonnard, and even Picasso can be characterized by their efforts to find a balance between those two extremes. Against this background, despite frequent periods of self-doubt, Vuillard remained committed to genre subjects taken from the modern everyday world and to an unsystematic technique based on sensation. His practical example was undoubtedly followed by younger artists – intermediaries between the Nabis and the Fauves such as Louis Valtat and Albert André – but he was never an artist who sought to attract pupils or disseminate ideas.

In the years 1900 and 1901 Vuillard spent time with Vallotton and Odilon Redon, both of whom in their different ways offered an alternative vision to the classical. While staying with Vallotton at Romanel in

49 *The Suitor* (K–X. Roussel and Marie Vuillard, rue Saint-Honoré). Dated 1893. Oil on cardboard, $12\frac{1}{2} \times 14\frac{7}{8}$ in. (31.8×36.4 cm.). Northampton, Massachusetts, Smith College Museum of Art

50 *Woman in Blue with Child* (Misia Natanson with Mimi Godebska, rue Saint-Florentin). 1899. Oil on cardboard, 19⅛ × 22¼ in. (48.6 × 56.5 cm.). Glasgow Art Gallery and Museum

Switzerland, Vuillard painted a number of fresh landscapes of the meadows and lakeside such as *Window on Lac Léman* (Plate 46). Vallotton's painting of 1903 of *Five Painters* (Plate 44), which situates Vuillard, Bonnard and Roussel in the company not only of Vallotton himself but also of Charles Cottet, suggests some sort of artistic regrouping. Vuillard seems to have drawn closer to Bonnard during these years. Together they made short trips abroad, to London in 1899 and to Spain in 1901, along with their new aristocratic patrons the Princes Bibesco. In Odilon Redon (Plate 47), with whom Vuillard stayed in the Gironde in 1901, he found a congenial companion whose independence, intelligence and poetic vision he respected, and whose recent experiments in pastel may have suggested new avenues he too could explore in terms of colour.

In 1901–2 Vuillard sketched out a large decorative panel, *Outbuildings at l'Etang-la-Ville* (Musée de Beauvais). Its arbitrary colouration – sugary pinks, dusty blues and greens woven together in tapestry-like texture – and lack of precision reveal an artist who could work with a considerable freedom of handling, indeed in this instance with an almost Redon-like fantasy. The destination of the panel is unknown, but the setting is once again the new suburban home of Ker and Marie Roussel; their daughter Annette is shown running through the grass in the foreground. From the time of her birth in 1898, Vuillard's much-loved niece was a favourite model.

As a confirmed bachelor, Vuillard's evident fondness for painting children deserves comment. His success was surely in large part due to his ability to remain detached, unsentimental and humorous. Yet being gentle and generous, he also seems to have had the gift of establishing an immediate rapport with his young sitters. Annette Vaillant, the daughter of the actress Marthe Mellot and Alfred Natanson (their introduction had been effected by Vuillard), recalled his arriving armed with exotic toys to entertain her while she sat for her portrait. Whereas friends gave a central place to images of their children – Denis casting his wife and family in biblical roles – Vuillard avoided such traditional iconography. Children slip into his images without dominating them. They are often seen from behind or above (Plates 33, 38), busily engaged in their own activities and discoveries. He recorded the developing relationship between Annette Roussel and her mother, father, grandmother and younger brother in a charming and truthful series of paintings. In one of the first, *The Roussel Family at Table* (Plate 52), she is brought as a babe in arms to the family meal, and can as yet be screened off with a newspaper. In *The Painter K–X. Roussel and his Daughter Annette* (Plate 59) of 1903, Vuillard uses his skill at catching character and mood through pose, placement and silhouette to convey the father's bemused and exhausted admiration of his beribboned and no doubt loquacious daughter. This painting exemplifies clearly a new feel for light and space on Vuillard's part, a point noted with approval by contemporary critics. The interior is airy rather than cramped. The harmonious unity is achieved by a consistent use of brilliant red and powdery blue across the whole surface.

Vuillard's acquisition of his first Kodak box camera can with reasonable certainty be dated to 1897. Thereafter he used it constantly and enthusiastically, and it is worth considering how this new passion affected his development as a painter. As in his paintings, he delighted in capturing on film informal get-togethers, conversations and cavortings, indoors and out, on holiday or in the privacy of the home. He had no interest in posed subjects or obvious picturesque views, but delighted in the *sur le vif* quality of the snapshot. He would appear to have made photographic records, rather as he made drawings, as *aides-mémoires* and as tools enabling him better to understand his subject. A photograph brought into focus the details of an interior. Around 1898, even in a still relatively flat painting, *Woman in Blue with Child* (Plate 50), showing Misia holding a baby aloft for admiration, we can see the beginnings of a more complex, all-embracing rather than reductive view of the subject. He faithfully observed the details of the cluttered setting, the wallpaper, tripod pedestal, screen and couch, as can be verified in his photograph of the same year (Plate 48). Vuillard was not an

51 *Misia in a Chaise Longue*. 1900. Distemper on cardboard, 23¾ × 24⅞ in. (60 × 62.7 cm.). Private Collection

52 *The Roussel Family at Table*. Dated 1899. Oil on cardboard, 23 × 36 in. (58 × 91 cm.). Private Collection

53 *Lucy Hessel in a Green Hat, Amfreville. c.* 1905. Oil on cardboard, 41½ × 30¾ in. (105.5 × 78 cm.). Saint Louis, Missouri, Joseph Pulitzer Jr.

artist who departed from reality into flights of fancy. But despite his unswerving fidelity to what he saw, the element of fantasy and inventiveness entered in at the level of emphasis, touch, and above all colour relationships. It was probably Thadée Natanson who wrote the account of *Woman in Blue* in 1908; he clearly considered it one of the gems of his collection:

> The frame holds in sufficient accentuated elements and enough invented relationships to enliven ten pictures or an important decoration. Only oriental carpets manage to weave together as many strident ideas and balance them in such a confined space. The reds are the only linking theme. The most strident chord is struck by a blue and a soft green which is set against a golden yellow, a dominant black and muted reds.

The still lifes and interiors painted after the turn of the century were no longer characterized by the ambiguities of form and space of which Vuillard was so fond earlier on. In a painting such as *Model undressing in the Studio, rue Truffaut* (Plate 56) of 1903, he represents space in a new, more realistic manner, indeed with something of the exaggeratedly wide-angle characteristic of the early fish-eye lens. One can discern a steady increase in his attention to the details of material objects, an attention which developed from a conscious *parti pris* to something of an obsession later on. In his journal, in 1921 or thereabouts, he picked up a key phrase from Paul Valéry: 'In execution there are no such things as details.' In its original context Valéry's words suggested that for creative artists the minutest details are just as important as the overall conception. Clearly the idea had a very direct relevance for Vuillard.

Around the turn of the century Vuillard's private life underwent a number of changes and shifts and a new era began. He witnessed the gradual separation and eventual divorce of his friends Misia and Thadée

54 Walter Richard Sickert: '*La Hollandaise*'. c. 1906. Oil on canvas, 20 × 15¾ in. (50.8 × 40 cm.). London, Tate Gallery

Natanson. Thadée was offered the chance to direct a coal mine in Hungary, a project whose practicality came as a welcome change from his somewhat ivory tower existence at *La Revue Blanche*, which in any case ceased publication in 1903. But the financial backing was provided by Alfred Edwards, a millionaire newspaper and theatre owner, who wished to pursue his new passion, Misia, unhindered. At various stages Misia rather heartlessly dragged Vuillard into the situation, but there is no hint of emotional turmoil in his portrait of her, *Misia in a Chaise Longue* (Plate 51), painted in Cannes in 1900, with its tranquil elegant Louis XV interior and tonality of sage greens and golden yellows.

After 1900 Misia, who became Madame Edwards in 1905, played a less prominent role in Vuillard's life. Her position as favourite model, muse and soulmate was taken up by another strong female figure, Lucy Hessel, wife of the picture dealer Jos Hessel, whom Vuillard had first met in 1895. Hessel worked for his uncle, Alexandre Bernheim, whose gallery in the rue Laffitte, later to move to the rue Richepanse, was fast becoming one of the most prominent and successful dealing in modern art in Paris. By 1900, Alexandre's sons, Josse and Gaston, had taken over the running of the firm and the gallery's name changed to Bernheim-Jeune. Not only was Vuillard scooped up by the gallery (he first showed work there in a group exhibition in 1900 and after 1906 had one-man shows on a regular basis), but by 1905 when he began his striking half-length portrait of Lucy in a stylish plumed hat (Plate 53), she and her husband had become powerful influences in his life. He called regularly at their apartment in the rue de Rivoli – an Aladdin's cave of contemporary art as Vuillard recorded in many pictures (Plate 57) – and was an amused and perceptive observer of their opulent lifestyle, not above joining in the occasional drawing-room game. For Jos Hessel, a gambler and member of the Jockey Club, art was another form of speculation, but he had the wit and foresight to see the quality of Vuillard's work before any other rival dealer and prided himself on the range of his personal collection of the artist's work.

Vuillard's intimate friendship with Lucy Hessel was to last some forty years, and has given rise to much

55 *Large Nude on a Couch.* 1911–12, reworked 1915–16. Distemper on paper laid down on canvas, 54⅜ × 49¼ in. (138 × 125 cm.). Zurich, Foundation E. G. Bührle Collection

56 *Model undressing in the Studio, rue Truffaut. c.* 1903. Oil on cardboard, 24½ × 35¼ in. (62 × 89 cm.). Fort Worth, Texas, Kimbell Art Museum

57 *Lucy Hessel in the Small Salon, rue de Rivoli.* 1903–4. Oil on cardboard, 29 × 25 in. (74 × 63.5 cm.). Private Collection

conjecture: but his journal, for so long inaccessible, seems to contain no great secrets about a relationship that for the most part was conducted under the public eye. The daughter of a rich Jewish textile merchant, Lucy Reiss had married Jos Hessel in the early 1890s, when he was still an impoverished journalist from Belgium. Despite Jos's inveterate philandering, Lucy never ceased to hold him dear. Jos Hessel would seem to have welcomed Vuillard as a third party who was able to console the wife whom he frequently neglected. It was in fact a mutually beneficial arrangement. Between Lucy Hessel and Vuillard there was a close bond of emotional dependence which could lead, as Annette Vaillant remembered, to volatile arguments. Vuillard relied on Lucy's encouragement of his work but was hypersensitive to her variable moods and state of health, and to the slightest hint of her disapproval. Perhaps he was discreet, but in his numerous paintings and drawings of her, Lucy comes across as a friend rather than a lover, a sensuous, forceful woman with a lively mind, discerning judgement and good sense of humour.

In the way that she dominated Vuillard's day-to-day existence and provided a focus for his art, Lucy Hessel gradually took over the role that had for so many years been performed by his mother, a situation that occasionally gave rise to difficulties and jealousies. While continuing to live at home, Vuillard allowed Lucy to organize the social side of his life, sometimes, one would have thought, to the point of distracting and dissipating his attention from the artistic projects he had in hand. Rarely, by mid-career, does his journal record a whole day spent concentrating exclusively on his work. More often, his periods in the studio were broken up by the arrival of visitors, lunch, tea or dinner engagements, a drive through the Bois or an outing to the theatre. At a period when Vuillard had numerous commissions for decorations as well as for portraits, between 1910 and 1914 for example, he would typically have three or more such projects on the go, working up each of them in short bursts of activity at different times of the day. Should an entirely new artistic idea occur to him, in the evening he would register it in his journal for future reference.

If an artist's graduation from the avant-garde to the establishment inevitably carries certain implications of *embourgeoisement*, in John Russell's view this was a fate that had befallen both Bonnard and Vuillard by 1905. After 1900 they both enjoyed a greater degree of financial security thanks to their arrangement with the Bernheim-Jeunes. Their works were also being seen at the major annual salons, a new departure in Vuillard's exhibiting practice. In 1903 the first-ever selective independent exhibition, the Salon d'Automne, was opened in Paris. It offset the now twenty-year-old unselective Salon des Indépendants, always held in the spring. Thereafter, Vuillard frequently sent groups of works to both exhibitions; in 1905, for instance, he was represented at the Salon d'Automne by an important group of decorative panels, the four painted for Dr Vaquez in 1896 and the pair painted for Schopfer in 1898 (Plates 42–3, 35–6). Since the panels had originally passed straight into the collections for which they were destined, this was a rare chance for the public and critics to assess Vuillard as a decorator. But it was the Fauve group who stole the show that year. It would be interesting to know how Vuillard responded to the works of Matisse and his friends. With some justification Maurice Denis, in his later writings, dismissed the furore around these artists' colouristic innovations, pointing out the equivalent sensation caused in the early 1890s by the Nabis's arbitrary colours. Vuillard too must surely have been reminded of his own early experiments when faced with the jangling palettes of the Fauves. In this context, the cultivatedly subdued tones of his decorations were in danger of taking on a fusty, period aura. For André Gide, however, who wrote a lengthy appraisal of the exhibition in the *Gazette des Beaux-Arts*, the juxtaposition with the Fauves' brash excesses lent Vuillard's more delicate colour sense an added charm: 'He never puts forward one colour without excusing it with a subtle and precious repetition. Too delicate to affirm, he insinuates, – an indescribable violet carmine in the two large "landscapes with figures" [the Schopfer panels] – but with such sureness that, while remaining surprising, this carmine

58 *Marthe Bonnard and her Dog, rue de Douai.*
Dated 1907. Oil on panel, 43 × 34¾ in. (109 × 88 cm.).
Melbourne, Australia, National Gallery of Victoria

nevertheless appears necessary.' Ironically in this year of the Fauvist colour revolution it was Vuillard who was judged 'one of the foremost colourists of our time' by François Monot in *Art et Décoration*. More than one critic drew analogies between Vuillard's colour use and the richness of oriental carpets, an analogy that is more frequently applied to Matisse; he was seen by most critics as a skilled, practised and subtle technician who belonged to a generation of artists who were now established and no longer at the forefront of experiment.

Not all the praise was unqualified, however. As if in defiance of his increasing attention to detail, Vuillard preserved a certain carelessness or 'negligence' in his technique. There are blank or roughly treated areas, not only in works that were evidently executed as studies but even in commissioned portraits like *M. and Mme Feydeau on a Sofa* (Plate 83) of 1901, that was delivered and paid for as a completed work. Here and elsewhere the warm neutral tones of the cardboard play an active part in the establishment of the colour relationships. It was a feature which perplexed certain fellow painters, Jacques-Emile Blanche for instance. And at an exhibition of Vuillard's work at the Bernheim-Jeune gallery in 1906, his old friends and mentors Marc Mouclier and Maurice Denis judged this 'butterfly' quality and Vuillard's refusal to finish to be something of an irritating affectation, with the implication that it was a passing phase.

If Vuillard's work was well represented and by and large well received in Paris in these years, his reputation outside France was also growing. In 1900 Octave Mirbeau penned a witty diatribe against the *retardataire* tastes of France's contemporary arts minister, pointing out that Vuillard and Bonnard, of whom the minister had not heard, were already being courted by enlightened collectors from abroad. Certainly they were being invited to participate in various international salons, the Secession groups of Vienna, Berlin and Brussels, for instance, and German museum directors were swifter to make purchases than their French counterparts. On a visit to Hamburg in 1913 both Vuillard and Bonnard were asked to paint portraits for the

59 *The Painter K.-X. Roussel and his Daughter Annette*. 1903. Oil on cardboard, 23 × 21 in. (58.2 × 53.1 cm.). Buffalo, New York, Albright-Knox Art Gallery

60 *Lucie Belin in the boulevard Malesherbes Studio.* 1915. Distemper on paper laid down on canvas, $51\frac{1}{8} \times 39\frac{3}{4}$ in. (130 × 101 cm.). Private Collection

Kunsthalle. Vuillard's *Cargo Boat at Hamburg* (Plate 45) was also painted during this visit. That year, too, Vuillard's work was included in the New York Armory Show, and in 1916 he sent two pictures, including the portrait of Lucie Belin (Plate 60), to a New York exhibition organized by the Lafayette Fund.

Knowledge of Vuillard's work in Britain was based mainly on his small, easily transported interiors, but the degree of interest shown is some indication of his standing there. Following his unpremeditated trip to London in 1892, Vuillard seems to have had fairly regular contact with British collectors, artists and exhibiting organizations. In 1898 and 1899, on the recommendation of the critic Théodore Duret, Vuillard and Bonnard were invited to participate in the first shows of the 'International Society of Painters, Sculptors and Engravers', an organization founded by Whistler and others with the aim of breaking down the hidebound prejudices and inward-looking nationalism of British art. They even travelled to London in 1899 to see their works hanging in the Skating Rink in Knightsbridge, an occasion which caused the exhibition secretary considerable embarrassment because both artists' works had been 'skyed', that is, hung so high as to be virtually invisible. They were evidently disconcerted by the dark, old-masterly tonality affected by so many of the British artists at that time.

It is tempting to suggest that by 1903–4 Vuillard felt an affinity with a British artist currently working in France, Walter Richard Sickert. A major Sickert one-man show was staged at the Bernheim-Jeune gallery in 1904. In the eyes of Jacques-Emile Blanche, an enthusiastic collector of the artist's work, Sickert's natural place was alongside Vuillard and Bonnard because of the similarity of his handling and subject-matter – theatre scenes and sombre modern interiors – and he regretted his absence from the Salon d'Automne that year. In 1905, Sickert indeed showed several works there.

Vuillard's renewed interest in painting nudes coincided with a general revival of interest in the nude among independent artists in Paris. He would undoubtedly have been familiar with the influential series of nudes Sickert painted in London around 1907–8 for several were exhibited shortly after completion at the Bernheim-Jeune gallery in Paris, among them '*La Hollandaise*' (Plate 54). Vuillard's own *Large Nude on a Couch* (Plate 55) of 1910, an unusually large-scale painting which Segard classified as a decoration, takes a similar interest in the foreshortened, natural, sensual pose favoured by Sickert; in both, the model is caught off her guard, and equivalent attention is given to the shabby decorative details and atmosphere of the room. But where Sickert's imagery carried overtones of the sleaziness of a London tenement, of violence and paid sex, Vuillard's characteristically more matter-of-fact, discreet and diffident approach made no attempt to depict more than an artist's studio, with the nude as a model taking a rest between sittings.

In his writings Sickert revealed himself to be a fervent admirer of Vuillard's talent; he ranked him, in 1910, above his great mentor Whistler, alongside Degas, as one of those masters one could learn from. Like some of his French contemporaries, he admitted to finding himself shocked at times by the seemingly slapdash, even violent means used by Vuillard, 'the scrawled splashes of distemper', but since they produced, from a distance, such a delicate and powerful effect, he reasoned that for Vuillard to have added another stroke would have been 'tautology and a distraction'. Such admiration was evidently shared by other future members of the Camden Town group. As early as 1908, when Louis Fergusson saw Harold Gilman's interiors of 'women sewing – women taking tea – women conversing in parlours', he was reminded simultaneously of 'Vermeer and Vuillard', comparisons which interestingly reveal the level of awareness of Vuillard's work among advanced artists in London. Sickert was highly critical of Roger Fry for omitting Vuillard from his so-called Post-Impressionist exhibition in 1910. Despite this omission, Vuillard was featured from time to time in British exhibitions and steadily if slowly has filtered into British private and public collections.

Chapter Four

VUILLARD AND THE THEATRE

The immense importance of theatre to Vuillard has long been recognized, particularly his close involvement with Lugné-Poe's Théâtre de l'Œuvre in the 1890s. During those years he worked in and for the theatre, designing playbills, illustrating programmes and painting stage sets. Of the latter no vestiges remain – being essentially makeshift and ephemeral, they would have been repainted many times before being discarded.

Like Sickert, Vuillard was an assiduous and absorbed theatre-goer throughout his career. Actors and playwrights were among his most intimate friends, and theatre people formed the dominant group among his patrons from the time of his very first commissions. In 1890, Lugné-Poe infected Vuillard with his own latest enthusiasm, pantomime; and that year Vuillard made a series of sketches of the highly successful pantomime *L'Enfant Prodigue*, performed at the Bouffes Parisiens (cf. Plate 61). Vuillard designed programmes and posters for the academic Conservatoire (Plate 22), where Lugné had been a student, and for the Théâtre Libre, where he was serving his apprenticeship. Lugné introduced Vuillard to his friend the critic Louis Malaquin, another Condorcet product, whose anti-establishment ideas did much to sever Lugné's ties with his teachers. Most important, Lugné gave Vuillard an introduction to the celebrated actor Coquelin Cadet. Although without much discrimination in taste, Coquelin was liberal with his purchases and commissions and readily offered to step in as the 'promoter' of Vuillard and Denis during Lugné's enforced absence from Paris on military service in the winter of 1890–1.

William Rothenstein, in his memoirs, recalled that around 1890 the Coquelin brothers had invited him and other fellow students from the Académie Julian to make sketches backstage at the Comédie Française. Vuillard had apparently jumped at the chance to earn a few francs in this way. Coquelin Cadet was particularly admired for the plasticity of his features, which were given their full comic possibilities by the plays of Molière, and a number of Vuillard's sketches showed him in Molière roles (Plate 139). Coquelin must have been impressed by Vuillard's extraordinarily daring caricatural watercolours, for he was eager to publicize and exhibit them. They were inspired, both in form and content, by the tradition of Japanese actor prints: that year a large exhibition of Japanese art at the Ecole des Beaux-Arts had excited the Nabis's interest.

Showing a recognized actor in character or star roles was a recognized line for another contemporary of Vuillard's who worked in the theatre, Toulouse-Lautrec. Vuillard, however, seems to have abandoned the genre as he became involved with the more obscure, highbrow developments in experimental theatre. During the period when he shared a studio with Lugné, he even had some say in the selection of plays. He was also fascinated by the atmosphere of the rehearsal room, absorbed by the whole mood of a play and its often makeshift performance.

61 *Pierrot Seated on a Chair*. 1890. Brush and Indian ink with white gouache on card, 12¼ × 9¼ in. (31 × 23.7 cm.). Private Collection

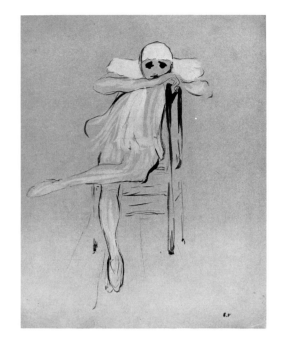

62 *Scene from Maeterlinck's 'L'Intruse' ('The Intruder')* (performed at the Théâtre d'Art on 20, 21 May 1891). Dated 1891. Oil on board, 11⅛ × 23⅞ in. (28 × 60.5 cm.). Location unknown

63 *L'Intruse (The Intruder)*. 1891. Brush and Indian ink on paper, 10⅞ × 20⅜ in. (27.5 × 51.5 cm.). Private Collection

The early 1890s were the years when French theatre first began to be infiltrated by Symbolist ideas. There was a growing campaign for an alternative to the current vogue for 'slice of life' naturalism epitomized by Antoine's Théâtre Libre, where a high degree of verisimilitude in the acting and the stage sets was pursued as an artistic goal. Paul Fort, the 'prince of poets', set up his Théâtre d'Art in late 1890 with grandiose and idealistic ambitions. He aimed at creating for an exclusive group of subscribers a theatre that would rise above the ugliness of everyday material reality to reach a higher order of poetic or psychological truth. There would be no call for carcasses of meat dripping blood on to the stage, but for suggestive sets in harmony with the mood of the drama. In the words of one of the young Symbolist playwrights, Pierre Quillard, the aim of a Symbolist set design was a 'simple décor that should be no more than an ornamental fiction, which completes the illusion of the drama through analogies of colours and lines'. This factor no doubt led to Paul Fort's choice of the Nabis, who were recognized as the contemporary painters most truly in tune with Symbolist ideas, as artistic contributors.

One of the first Théâtre d'Art productions to make an impact on Vuillard was *L'Intruse*, a one-act play by Maurice Maeterlinck, staged as part of an ambitious mixed entertainment at the Vaudeville on 20 and 21 May 1891. Vuillard was inspired to produce a painting on the same theme, which he exhibited at the first-ever Nabi exhibition at Saint-Germain-en-Laye in 1891 (Plate 62). As specified in Maeterlinck's stage directions, the setting was a room in a château, with French doors opening on to a terrace and garden and no fewer than three other doors opening on to adjacent rooms. Various sketches by Vuillard of this set survive: in two of them a clock is prominent (Plate 63), for the play deals with the tensions of a family waiting, hovering between two sick rooms where a mother and her recently delivered child lie dying. Six performers are clearly indicated by Vuillard, seated stage left around a table and a faltering lamp. Attention is focused on the blind grandfather (played by Lugné), whose unseeing eyes are the only ones to perceive the arrival in their midst of the invisible 'intruder', Death.

The morbid themes of sickness and brooding that pervaded Maeterlinck's subsequent plays, *Les*

64 *Mme Vuillard at Home* (loose sheet from the Album Saint-Honoré). 1894. Pen and ink and watercolour on paper, 8¼ × 8¼ in. (20.7 × 20.7 cm.). Private Collection

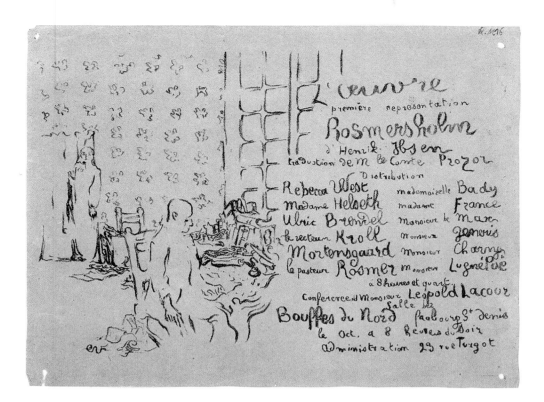

65 *Programme for Ibsen's 'Rosmersholm'.* 1893. (For the Théâtre de l'Œuvre.) Lithograph, 8¼ × 12¼ in. (21 × 31 cm.). Paris, Bibliothèque Nationale

66 *Programme for Bjornsen's 'Beyond Human Strength'.* 1894. (For the Théâtre de l'Œuvre.) Lithograph, 12¼ × 18½ in. (31 × 47 cm.). Paris, Bibliothèque Nationale

67 *Mme Vuillard and her Daughter – La Causette. c.* 1892. Oil on canvas, 12½ × 15½ in. (31.5 × 39.2 cm.). Edinburgh, Scottish National Gallery of Modern Art

68 *Large Interior with Six Figures.* Dated 1897. Oil on canvas, 34¾ × 76¼ in. (88 × 193 cm.). Zurich, Kunsthaus

69 *A Theatre Corridor with Toulouse-Lautrec. c.* 1894. Oil on canvas, 10⅛ × 8¼ in. (26.5 × 21 cm.). Private Collection

Aveugles, *Pelléas et Mélisande* and *Intérieur*, in all of which Lugné appeared, can be said to characterize several of Vuillard's early interiors in which figures are shown asleep, or sick, in bed, or hovering in half-open doorways (Plates 12, 49, 67). The way in which Vuillard's figures gradually emerge from the shadows, their presence uncertain, ambiguous amid the overlapping shapes and muffled tonalities of their surroundings (Plates 30, 64), may be attributable to those experimental productions at the Théâtre d'Art in which the actors were often only partially visible to the audience. There are plenty of contemporary accounts, not all of them complimentary, of the slow pace and stilted movements, of the sparse, repetitive dialogue and of the dimly-lit, rudimentary sets to suggest that these were typical features of Symbolist theatre. Lugné's style of acting, which earned him the nickname of the 'somnambulist', although appropriate to Maeterlinck, whose other-worldly plays were recognized as being awkward to stage, was controversial when applied to the more naturalistic plays and dialogue of Ibsen, Strindberg and Bjornson.

In the 1890s Lugné was to dedicate himself to introducing Parisian audiences to the new wave of Scandinavian drama, in particular Ibsen, and later counted this as the greatest achievement of his company, the Théâtre de l'Œuvre, which he founded in 1893. Vuillard, who was one of the co-directors, is said to have suggested the theatre's name. At first most critics complained of the importation of 'Northern fogs' and of the overriding air of gloom at L'Œuvre, so alien to French taste, but by the latter half of the 1890s Lugné's act of faith had been vindicated and his company was well and truly launched. Lugné transformed Ibsen into a hero of Symbolism, interpreting his plays as near actionless 'drames d'intérieur'. As such they had an obvious kinship with Vuillard's actionless interiors. Vuillard was called upon to design the programme and the décor for the first new production at L'Œuvre in October 1893, Ibsen's *Rosmersholm*. His programme design (Plate 65) shows the pastor, Rosmer, seated at his disarrayed desk, seemingly transfixed by his loss of faith and inability to act. His programme for Bjornson's *Au-dessus des forces humaines* (*Beyond Human Strength*) (Plate 66), another play concerned with the uncertain position of religion in modern society, deployed a dramatic design using the full potential of black lithographic ink for chiaroscuro effects. A more light-hearted note was struck by his advertisement for *La Revue Blanche* which appeared on the back cover, demonstrating how closely the readership of the Natansons' journal coincided with the subscription audience at L'Œuvre.

The printing of these programmes, using a single colour, would have been straightforward and cheap, no doubt an important factor given the shaky financial footing on which L'Œuvre operated. The same concern to cut costs determined the simplified backdrops, painted in the *à la colle* technique by Vuillard and his friends, which were sufficiently generalized to serve for more than one production. These backdrops not only introduced Vuillard to the properties and advantages of *colle*, they also offered the Nabis their first opportunity to paint decorations on a monumental scale. One is safe to assume that there were no details or clearcut architectural lines. Indeed so indeterminate was Vuillard's backdrop for the last act of Ibsen's *Master Builder* that a stage carpenter in London tried to hang it upside down. (Lugné-Poe and his company were staging their first English tour in March 1895.) The carpenter confided to Alfred Sutro, the Symbolist playwright and translator who was responsible for introducing Lugné to English audiences: 'I've tried that cloth both ways and it don't make sense either way.' Sutro sorted out the problem and reported that from the stalls Vuillard's scene was 'curiously effective'. Sutro's name appears several times in Vuillard's journal during the 1890s. He bought some small-scale interiors from the painter and later played host to him when Vuillard came to England.

While it would be misleading to suggest that the seriousness with which the Northern dramatists probed social and moral issues was paralleled in Vuillard's work, there is no doubt that his representations of figures in interiors in the 1890s borrowed something of the portentous mood of Symbolist drama (Plates 64,

70 Photograph by Jacques Salomon. Vuillard sketching from his window, 6 place Vintimille. *c*. 1935–40. Paris, Antoine Salomon

67); moreover, his visual use of dramatic lighting, partly inspired by stage effects, was surely intended to suggest, with a similar intensity to Lugné's productions, the workings of the inner life. Alfred Jarry's account of Vuillard's set design for Hauptmann's *Les Ames Solitaires* evokes 'the semi-gloom given off by green lamps on red tables where Vuillard has lit up the vegetative life that make Kaethe's hands look so pale'. The design recalls closely the lamplight effects and colour contrasts in some of his early interiors (Plate 76). As it happened, only the dress rehearsal of Hauptmann's play took place, in December 1893. Suspicion about the allegedly radical politics of the translator led to further performances being banned by the police on a trumped-up charge, an indication of the general panic about anarchist outrages which prevailed at the time.

As well as his intellectual and practical involvement with high Symbolist drama of the early 1890s, Vuillard clearly also enjoyed and found artistic stimulus in theatre as a social occasion. Some rather garbled notes in his journal for 7 November 1894 hint at this, and give an insight into the artist's creative processes:

Yesterday afternoon Lerolle and his sister-in-law – the calm impression given by these likeable people, reserved but congenial, not too many trifling matters. Set that against the evening at Lugné's theatre – all those sensual Jewesses, their silks shimmering in the shadows. Think about pictures that oppose one another in expression. Think about *Anabella* [an adaptation by Maeterlinck of John Ford's *'Tis Pity She's a Whore*] set against the scene in the studio with Lerolle, or again at the theatre in the red corridors Lerolle and Puvis/Anquetin Lautrec.

A painting which is usually taken to represent *A Theatre Corridor with Toulouse-Lautrec* (Plate 69) must surely date from this occasion. One assumes that what struck and amused Vuillard was the chance conjunction, in a confined space, of two upright and dignified establishment artists and two disreputable extrovert artists-about-town. However, although humorous and lively, the picture is so simplified as to be barely legible, and apart from the unmistakable stunted silhouette of Lautrec in the left foreground, it is

71 *Place Vintimille*. 1911. Five-panel screen for Miss Chapin. Distemper on paper laid down on canvas, each panel 102⅜ × 23⅝ in. (230 × 60 cm.). New York, Private Collection

72, 73 *Place Vintimille*. 1909–10. Two panels, for Henry Bernstein. Distemper on cardboard mounted on canvas, left: 78¾ × 27¾ in. (200 × 69.5 cm.); right: 78¾ × 27½ in. (200 × 69.9 cm.). New York, Guggenheim Museum, Justin K. Thannhauser Collection

74, 75 *Streets of Paris: Rue de Calais* and *Place Vintimille*. 1909–10. Two panels for Henry Bernstein. Distemper on cardboard mounted on canvas, each 78¾ × 19⅝ in. (200 × 49 cm.). Private Collection.

76 *Under the Lamp*. Dated 1892. Oil on canvas, 12¼ × 15¾ in. (31.1 × 40 cm.). Saint-Tropez, Musée de L'Annonciade

77 *The Bernheim-Jeune Brothers and their Wives, avenue Henri-Martin.* Dated 1905. Oil on cardboard, 22½ × 28½ in. (57 × 72.5 cm.). Paris, Bernheim-Jeune Collection

78 *'Sunny Morning', Lucy Hessel and Denise Natanson in the garden at Les Pavillons, Villerville.*
Dated 1910. Distemper on canvas, 78 × 56 in. (203 × 142 cm.). London, Private Collection

79 *The Haystack*. 1907–8, reworked 1930–40. One of a pair of panels for Prince Bibesco. Distemper on canvas, 92½ × 65 in. (235 × 165 cm.). Dijon, Musée des Beaux-Arts (Dépot des Musées nationaux)

80 *Annette in Mme Vuillard's Room, rue de Calais. c.* 1916. Oil on cardboard, 22 × 28⅜ in. (56 × 72 cm.). Private Collection

81 Photograph by Vuillard. Lucy Hessel at Amfreville looking at her portrait (Plate 53). *c.* 1905. Paris, Antoine Salomon

82 Photograph by Vuillard. Vuillard's mother in the rue de Calais apartment, looking at one of his paintings (Plate 80). *c.* 1916. Paris, Antoine Salomon

difficult to make identifications with any certainty. The notes are revealing in a more general sense. If the calm, reserved atmosphere created by people like the Lerolles, artistic patrons and members of the *haute bourgeoisie* intelligentsia, was the one in which Vuillard felt most at home – these same qualities, after all, characterized so many of his early interiors – he was also fascinated by the more exuberant, luxurious world he associated with the aristocratic Lautrec and with the 'sensual Jewesses'. It is tempting to think that Vuillard continued to cultivate and exploit the dramatic tension of 'pictures that oppose one another in expression' in his later interiors; one thinks of the marked contrast between the frugal air of his own apartments and the colourful richness of the Hessels' (Plates 130, 90).

Although Vuillard's active commitment to L'Œuvre seems to have diminished after 1895, the experience of making theatre was not forgotten. Its influence can arguably be seen in his lasting aptitude for constructing effective *mises-en-scène*, for assembling a group in an interior setting so that it worked as a dramatic tableau as well as a decorative ensemble. Once he began to re-introduce the third dimension, a consistent feature of his interiors after 1900, it was often a stage-like space that he represented; the apparently casual positions of the figures within that space are in fact carefully thought out with a stage-director's eye (Plates 3, 68, 77). The First World War interior, *Annette in Mme Vuillard's Room* (Plate 80), is a particularly striking example. Many of his cityscapes, especially those painted for Henry Bernstein and Marguerite Chapin (Plates 93–6, 71), have something of the insubstantial artifice of stage sets, with anonymous figures, young and old, working and at leisure, coming and going under the shifting skies and trees whose foliage marks the seasons' change.

Outings to the theatre were the chief form of entertainment of Vuillard's circle. Vuillard's own tastes were fairly catholic, ranging from classical concerts and drama to the circus, but by the early 1900s he was more likely to be found at the popular bourgeois comedies that formed the staple repertoire of the boulevard theatre than at marginal avant-garde plays. He never missed the first nights of plays written or produced by his friends, or those in which friends of his were appearing. In fact it was not unusual for him to go to the theatre

83 *M. and Mme Feydeau on a Sofa.* 1901. Distemper on cardboard, 18⅛ × 30¾ in. (46 × 78 cm.). Private Collection

84 *Pot of Flowers in the Studio, rue Truffaut.* 1901–2. Oil on cardboard, 19 × 24½ in. (48.5 × 62 cm.). Edinburgh, Scottish National Gallery of Modern Art

85 Sketch for *Denise and Annette Natanson at Saint-Jacut*. 1909. Pencil on paper, 6 × 3⅞ in. (15.2 × 9.8 cm.). Private Collection

three times a week. His close theatrical friends included actresses such as Marthe Mellot, whose career lasted from her début with L'Œuvre well into the twentieth century when she took roles in more mainstream theatre, and playwrights such as Alfred Athis (the *nom de plume* used by Alfred Natanson, Marthe Mellot's husband, when he took to writing plays), Romain Coolus, Pierre Véber and Tristan Bernard.

The stage people Vuillard met through the Hessels were more often than not highly successful vaudeville celebrities. Georges Feydeau, a great amateur art enthusiast, was a regular client of the Bernheim-Jeune gallery, often to be found there at the end of an afternoon. Perhaps it is such an occasion that Vuillard caught in his gently satirical portrait (Plate 83), in which Feydeau appears to be holding forth, cigar in teeth, under the amused but benevolent eye of his wife. It was probably the Bibescos who were responsible for introducing the scabrous and swashbuckling playwright Henry Bernstein to Vuillard's work. Bernstein bought Vuillard's early Coquelin caricatures (see Plate 139) among other works, and then acquired the *Streets of Paris* panels (Plates 72–3, 93–6) between 1908 and 1910. In the year when he first came into contact with Vuillard, Bernstein was a controversial figure. His play *Israël*, first staged in October 1908, which set out to expose the anti-Semitism still rife in Parisian society, caused such a public outcry that performances were curtailed. Interestingly enough, the élite moneyed clientèle that Vuillard's work attracted was predominantly Jewish. Vuillard himself seems to have felt something of an alien in what he saw as the 'sensual' Jewish milieu, although it also had a hypnotic fascination for him.

Romain Coolus and Tristan Bernard were both intimates of the Hessels, often part of the company during the long summer *villégiatures*; Bernard eventually married Lucy's close friend, her cousin Marcelle Aron. Having served his apprenticeship in the 1890s with the avant-garde Théâtre de l'Œuvre, Bernard built up a successful reputation in vaudeville in the twentieth century and was gradually assimilated into the bourgeois establishment. Exactly the same social environment provided the raw material for Bernard's and

86 *Denise and Annette Natanson at Saint-Jacut.* 1909. Distemper on paper laid down on canvas, 33¼ × 30¾ in. (84 × 78 cm.). Leningrad, Hermitage (Photograph Bernheim-Jeune)

Coolus's craft as it did for Vuillard's and there are interesting links to be made between the type of theatre they produced and certain new developments in the subject-matter of Vuillard's paintings. The artistic potential of the city dwellers' weekend or holiday in the country or by the sea escaped neither painter nor playwright. Indeed a degree of parallelism was inescapable. Annette Vaillant recalled a summer holiday in 1909, spent at Saint-Jacut in Normandy, when Vuillard would be busy painting in one room (Plates 85, 86) while in another her father, Alfred Natanson, and Tristan Bernard were collaborating on their new play, *Le Costaud des Epinettes*. Of course the approaches and conventions of representation were different. The satirical plays of Coolus and Bernard brought up to date with new psychoanalytical twists the well-tried formulae of French bourgeois comedy. Love and intrigue, complicated by the social barriers and class differences that underlay that apparently untroubled era of the Belle Epoque, inevitably became the playwrights' dominant themes, for all Bernard's earlier determination to avoid those 'eternal stories of adultery'. Vuillard seems to have been able to observe the guests' comings and goings, groupings and regroupings, from more of a distance, with a gentler humour and a greater degree of detachment. His decorative compositions, whether fluid exterior views or more structured interiors, do no more than hint, by the arrangement of figures into courting couples or conversation pieces, at the potential for dramatic intrigue (Plates 35, 36, 41, 78).

The significance of Tristan Bernard for Vuillard was not just as a friend who appeared frequently in his society paintings (Plates 41, 79). It was Bernard's hugely successful play *Le Petit Café*, first performed at the Palais-Royal in October 1911, that was chosen by Vuillard as the subject of one of his decorations for the new Théâtre des Champs-Elysées. Plans to build a new modern theatre in the most fashionable quarter of Paris were launched in 1911. The brainchild of Gabriel Astruc, the Théâtre des Champs-Elysées was to be a 'Temple of Art' where the latest in music, dance and drama could be presented under the most favourable conditions. The project was heralded as the most important and ambitious undertaking of its kind since Garnier's Opéra in the 1870s. It brought together some of the most innovative ideas in architecture and interior design; Henry Van de Velde played an important role and the Perret brothers used reinforced concrete for the first time ever in a public building.

The overall style of the theatre, from its façade on the avenue Montaigne to its main auditorium, had a strong neo-classical orientation, and this was picked up in the decorative paintings of Denis, Roussel and Lebasque as well as in sculptural bas relief friezes by Bourdelle. Maurice Denis's task was to decorate the cupola with four enormous friezes celebrating the histories of Music and Dance (Plate 87). By comparison, Vuillard's contribution was modest. In May 1912 he was commissioned to produce decorative panels for the foyer of the Comédie, a small pretty gilt theatre within a theatre, situated above the main entrance hall on the sixth floor and destined to present, in the words of Maurice Guillemot, critic for *Art et Décoration*, 'a repertoire of light comedy, where the Parisian and boulevardier public will be delighted to find plays exactly suited to its frivolity and habitual inattention.' Unlike Roussel, whose commissioned stage curtain took the classical theme of *Bacchus's Cortège*, Vuillard made no concessions to the general, timeless classicism of the decorative programme. His two panels on the theme of Comedy, supplemented by a series of smaller panels and overdoors, were decidedly up to date and painted in a bright colourful palette, similar to the Bois-Lurette panels painted that same year (Plate 91). Bernard's *Le Petit Café* dealt with the amusing complications in the life of a café waiter following his unexpected receipt of a windfall. Vuillard used a scene from the second act, where the protagonists meet in a smart restaurant, to exemplify 'modern comedy' (Plate 89). For the complementary decorative panel 'classical comedy' he chose a scene from Molière's *Le Malade Imaginaire*. In both he introduced witty naturalistic details, such as the rows of spectators' heads.

This direct involvement with theatre design had a sequel some twenty-five years later. Vuillard, Denis, Roussel and Bonnard were among the many artists commissioned by the State to paint panels for the new Théâtre de Chaillot, one of the showpieces of the Universal Exhibition of 1937, sited on the heights of the Trocadéro. The stark modernism of the theatre's architecture scarcely provided a sympathetic setting for decorative paintings, particularly for Vuillard's design, a somewhat baroque fantasy, once again on the theme of Comedy (Plate 137). But the whole commission seems to have fallen foul of bureaucratic ineptitude. Vuillard was not given the information he sought about the dimensions or the setting and was dismayed, when eventually allowed on to the site, to discover his panel was to be hung above a doorway. Uncharacteristically, he had chosen to evoke comedy in an allegorical way, incorporating characters from Shakespeare and Molière into a landscape setting. Against all the odds, however, Vuillard's decorative sense triumphed, and he produced a work which, according to Claude Roger-Marx, was 'in the best tradition of mural painting'.

The cross-fertilization between play and painting in Vuillard's commissioned decorations for the Théâtre de Champs-Elysées was rare. In general, his theatrical experience informed his paintings in less obvious ways. In the design for sets for bourgeois comedy, the greatest importance was attached to detail, to the matching of exactly the right props to a particular social milieu, to identifying a character's tastes through his possessions (a far cry from those bare, suggestive sets Vuillard helped with in the 1890s). A similar belief in the telling power of detail seems to have underlain Vuillard's development of an ever-increasing exactitude in his interiors and portraits after 1910 or so. In *The Visit* (Plate 90), not only does the choice of possessions immediately identify his sitters as *mondaines bourgeoises*, the *mise-en-scène* could almost have been transplanted from a bourgeois comedy. Interestingly, this closeness worked both ways, for paintings by Vuillard were sometimes used as part of the décor of a play set. On one occasion, in the 1920s, a Vuillard still life lent by Hessel was hung in a stage set at the Comédie Française; for the playwright, Paul Géraldy, it was a way 'of being precise about the tone of the people living there and also . . . of paying discreet homage to Vuillard'.

DV CŒVR DE L'HOMME DE TOVTES LES VOIX DE LA NATVRE JAILLIT LA DIVINE SYMPHONIE

87 Maurice Denis: *Symphony*. One of
four panels from the Cupola of the
Théâtre des Champs-Elysées. 1912–13.
Width *c.* 13 m. Paris, Théâtre des
Champs-Elysées

88 Ker-Xavier Roussel: *The Birth of
Venus*. 1910. One of three panels for
Jean Schopfer. Oil on canvas. Location
unknown

89 *'Le Petit Café'*. One of the decorative panels in the Foyer of the Comédie des Champs-Elysées. Dated 1913. Distemper on canvas, $70\frac{7}{8} \times 110\frac{1}{4}$ in. (180 × 280 cm.). Paris, Théâtre des Champs-Elysées

90 *In the Hessels' Salon, Evening, rue de Naples,* or *The Visit*. 1938. Distemper on canvas, 39⅜ × 53¾ in. (100 × 136.5 cm.). Washington, DC, National Gallery of Art

91 Overleaf *The Veranda at Loctudy in Brittany*. Left: *Lucy Hessel and Denise Notansom*; right: *Two Women Embroidering*. 1912. The door surround in its original setting in the Bernheim-Jeune's Normandy villa Bois-Lurette. The panels were dismantled and reworked after the villa was sold. Distemper on canvas, existing panels measure (left) 78¾ × 44 in. (200 × 112 cm.). Josefowitz Collection; (right) 79½ × 44¼ in. (201 × 113.5 cm.). Paris, Musée d'Orsay. Photograph Bernheim-Jeune

Chapter Five

CITY AND COUNTRY:
DECORATIVE PROJECTS AND WAR WORK

In 1904 Vuillard and his mother left the rue Truffaut in the Batignolles for the rue de la Tour in Passy. The move to Passy, a more airy, almost provincial tree-lined quarter, seems to have inspired Vuillard to exploit the motifs he could find immediately outside his window. In about 1906 he painted a large horizontal panel of the gardens, greenhouses and backs of houses he could see from his apartment in the rue de la Tour (Plate 92) – a view that had already been hemmed in by new construction since his arrival. The first of his series of vertical-format street scenes acquired by Henry Bernstein, the *Streets of Paris* (Plates 93–6), also date from this period. In one we have a direct view up the street towards the Eiffel Tower. In 1908 the Vuillards moved back to Clichy, to an apartment on the corner of the rue de Calais and the small residential square, place Vintimille (now place Adolphe-Max). There they would remain, first on the fourth floor, then on the second, until the building's redevelopment forced them in 1926 to move fifty yards to a more modern apartment with a different view on to the square.

The place Vintimille formed the subject of the second set of the *Streets of Paris* (Plates 72–3). These vertiginous perspectives, some seen from street level, others from an upper window, were unprecedented in Vuillard's own work. Although conceived on a different scale and for a different purpose, they make an interesting comparison with the illustrations of Parisian street life by artists such as Steinlen. Vuillard's many decorative panels of the place Vintimille include an ambitious folding screen (Plate 71), produced in 1911 for Marguerite Chapin (Plate 102). In order that the screen should unfold with a panorama of the whole square, he adopted a broad perspective, more than could be encompassed by the human eye. (To assist him with the composition he took several photographs of the square from a single spot.) Such works echo his earlier delight in observing the spectacle of the public gardens. Indeed, he noted that it was his retouching of the *Public Gardens* series (Plates 32, 33) in 1908 that sparked off his renewed interest in the theme.

If Vuillard's views of the city sometimes came to resemble those of the Impressionists before him (he was struck by 'souvenirs de Monet' in December 1909 as he tried to envisage the composition of his second series, commissioned by Bernstein), they preserved a more personal ingredient of wit and intimate engagement that was his alone. The two large decorations of the place Saint-Augustin, painted in 1912, took their viewpoints from a pavement café, across empty tables, encompassing the wide open space of the busy junction and the wedges of Haussmann apartment blocks which marked the openings of the axial boulevards. Although *The Soda Syphon* (Plate 98) is directly comparable to Bonnard's *Place Clichy* (Plate 97), painted the previous year (even to the style of the women's hats, the positioning of the café tables and awning), where Bonnard minimized depth by introducing a flat frieze of passers-by in the foreground, Vuillard left his

92 *View from the Artist's Window, rue de la Tour. c.* 1906. Distemper on paper laid down on canvas, 28 × 61⅞ in. (71.5 × 157.5 cm.). Milwaukee Art Center (Gift of Mr and Mrs Harry L. Bradley)

93, 94, 95, 96 Overleaf *Streets of Paris: The Eiffel Tower; The Street; Child in the Gutter; The Watering-Cart.* Dated 1908–10. Four of a series of eight panels, acquired by Henry Bernstein. Distemper on paper laid down on canvas, smaller panels: 76¾ × 17¾ in. (195 × 45 cm.); larger panels: 76¾ × 25⅝ in. (195 × 65 cm.). Private Collection

foreground clear of human interest, focusing the viewer's attention on the busy street traders in the middle ground and then drawing it on into deeper space by a dextrous use of patches of colour and shadow. Despite, even militating against, the complexity of the composition and its convincing illusion of depth, Vuillard's technique of *peinture à la colle* remained remarkably splashy and free, just as Sickert had observed, with areas of coarse impasto in the middle ground (Plate 99).

Another main theme in Vuillard's work before the First World War, one which again harked back to the Impressionists' interests in the 1860s and 1870s, was that of the Parisian bourgeoisie at leisure. He was not idle when he joined the Hessels' summer house parties at their chosen *villégiature*, sometimes in Brittany but more usually somewhere on the fashionable Normandy coast, 'so close to Paris and so far from the sea' as Reynaldo Hahn quipped. It was at Amfreville in Normandy, where they stayed each summer from 1905 to 1907, that Vuillard worked on the large portrait of Lucy (Plate 53). While there, he took a number of snapshots of his companions, including one of Lucy passing judgement on her portrait (Plate 81). Back in his studio in Paris, with a decorative commission from Prince Emmanuel Bibesco for two panels (*The Haystack* and *The Avenue of Trees*), he was to turn to these holiday snapshots. *The Haystack* (Plate 79) was based on a photograph of Lucy and Marcelle Aron, but Vuillard incorporated into his painting the figure of Tristan Bernard from another photograph of friends sitting on a beach. This use of photographs rather than drawings as a starting-point was a procedure Vuillard noted in his journal. It clearly had drawbacks in terms of his ability

97 Pierre Bonnard: *Place Clichy*. 1912. Oil on canvas, 54⅜ × 80 in. (138 × 203 cm.). Besançon, Musée des Beaux-Arts et d'Archéologie

98 *Place Saint-
Augustin. The Soda
Syphon.* 1912–13. One
of a pair of panels.
Distemper on paper
laid down on canvas,
$61\frac{1}{2} \times 76$ in. (156×193
cm.). Private Collection

99 Detail of Plate 98

to achieve tonal and colouristic unity. When, some years later, he confronted the panels, they were hanging in the same room as his earlier Villeneuve decorations painted for Schopfer (Plates 35, 36). The juxtaposition was to the detriment of the later panels and Vuillard judged them severely: he noted that they appeared heavy, the colours dark, the tonal values uninteresting – failings that he tried to correct through retouching.

In contrast to *The Haystack*, the seascapes and beach scenes Vuillard painted in 1908 at Le Pouliguen in southern Brittany and in 1909 at Saint-Jacut on the Channel coast (Plates 103, 104) are characterized by a blonder palette, a sureness and lightness of touch, and a remarkable freedom. In his seascape of 1909 (Plate 104) for instance, the relatively painterly treatment of the sea and sky contrasts with the playful flat treatment of the rocks in the foreground. Amid the swirls of grey, patterned with flecks and striations of white, one only gradually becomes aware of the presence of the woman, probably Lucy Hessel, lying under a parasol. Similarly, in *Woman reading in the Reeds, Saint-Jacut* (Plate 138), a careful balancing of blank paper with long undisguised brushstrokes was sufficient to suggest the spiky sea grass, the sand, even the salt breeze. Rather than the rural visions of a painter attuned to the earth and to the close observation of nature, these are the rarefied landscape visions of the city dweller on holiday. As a painter entirely in command of his medium (and *peinture à la colle* is noted for its intractability), Vuillard was able to execute them swiftly, during those inspired flashes of energy of which he had spoken diffidently to Denis. Such studies must have been a welcome change from the more prolonged concentration required for the many series of decorative panels he produced during these years. With their blond colouring and judicious use of tonal values, they belonged to a tradition that encompassed Corot and Berthe Morisot, both of whom Vuillard greatly admired.

A talent for seascapes was one of the many attributes Vuillard shared with the fictional painter Elstir, the creation of Marcel Proust. The first volume of Proust's *A la Recherche du temps perdu* was published in 1912 and subsequent volumes continued to appear at intervals until 1927, after the author's death. The literary portrait of Elstir was constructed from a composite of the painters Proust admired, including Turner, Manet, Monet, Whistler and Degas. However, the details of his mode of living, working and talking were more closely based on artists Proust knew in the 1900s, notably Paul Helleu, Jacques-Emile Blanche, Sickert and Vuillard, all of whom worked on the Channel coast. Proust probably knew Vuillard through *La Revue Blanche* as well as through their mutual friends the Bibescos; he clearly admired his art and his intelligence, and their correspondence on the subject of Vermeer perhaps bore fruit in the character of Charles Swann.

In 1907, while Proust was staying at the fashionable resort of Cabourg in Normandy (the original of his fictional Balbec), he visited Vuillard in nearby Amfreville and was evidently struck by the artist's down-to-earth practicality. Vuillard dressed for painting in workmen's overalls and had a throwaway manner of referring to the Old Masters in conversation: 'A chap like Giotto, don't you think, or even a chap like Titian, knew just as much as Monet . . .' With the points of reference disguised, these words would turn up in Elstir's speech some twenty years later. At a more general level, Proust's literary undertaking, a nostalgic panoramic picture of an era that was doomed to disappear, was a project in many ways comparable to Vuillard's *oeuvre* taken as a whole. Both writer and artist were attracted by the same ephemeral aspects of the social milieu in which they lived – the fashions, the meeting-places, the private interiors and their changing decorative styles. In Vuillard's portraits and group portraits, especially those painted from 1909–10 onwards, his attention to details of dress and setting reveals as much about the way his sitters lived as his attention to physiognomy reveals about their character. Just as the dramatis personae in *A la Recherche du temps perdu* appear and reappear, evolving over a protracted time-span, so in Vuillard's paintings the same models are featured again and again: children grow up, marry and leave home, Lucy Hessel's hair turns grey, memories are evoked as one era succeeds another (Plates 78, 112, 109, 90).

100 *The Library*. Dated 1911; reworked 1914. Decorative panel for Miss Chapin. Distemper on canvas, 157½ × 118⅛ in. (400 × 300 cm.). Paris, Musée d'Orsay

101 *Annette Daydreaming. c.* 1915. Distemper on paper laid down on canvas, $29\frac{1}{8} \times 27\frac{1}{2}$ in. (74 × 70 cm.). Private Collection

102 *Miss Marguerite Chapin with her Fox-Terrier*. Dated 1910. Oil on cardboard, $23\frac{1}{4} \times 29$ in. (59 × 73.6 cm.). Cambridge, Fitzwilliam Museum

Throughout his career as a decorator, Vuillard worked mainly for private clients. One of his more intense periods of commissioned work, between 1910 and 1911, brought him briefly into the orbit of Marguerite Chapin, a wealthy young American who had come to Paris to develop her singing voice, but delighted in collecting around her a phalanx of talented young writers. As well as the folding screen representing *Place Vintimille* (Plate 71) and a delightful informal portrait, really a study of her cluttered but exquisitely harmonious salon (Plate 102), Vuillard was commissioned to paint a huge decoration, *The Library* (Plate 100), for her gracious ground-floor apartment in the rue de l'Université. In the right foreground he placed his patron's slim silhouette, thrown into relief by the light, presumably electric, behind her. She appears to be taking tea with a group of her literary friends. In the final, reworked state of the image, the use of such harsh lighting, underlining the modernity of the setting in the lower third of the panel, makes a rather unsatisfactory contrast with the more muted colouring and the more traditional taste represented in the composition's central and upper sections, where a Gobelins tapestry based on Titian's *Adam and Eve* hangs beneath a classical bas-relief frieze.

This commission, on which he embarked in late 1910, seems to have caused Vuillard considerable trouble. Such self-conscious references to art of the past were a new departure for him. Were they perhaps made in deference to his patron or at her request, for she was still in the process of deciding on the decoration of the room in which the panel was to hang? He made numerous visits to the Louvre, to examine the tapestries and the classical sculpture, and he made copies in the Musée de Sculpture Comparée at the Trocadéro so as to get the details of the bas-relief right. But shortly after the panel was completed and delivered to the apartment in the rue de l'Université, Miss Chapin decided she did not want it after all. Simultaneously, to her friends' surprise and Vuillard's consternation, for he had become infatuated with her, she announced her marriage to an Italian aristocrat, which earned her the title Princess Caetani de Bassiano. Vuillard was left with an enormous and unwieldy panel on his hands. It was exhibited at Bernheim-Jeune's in April 1912 and bought the following year by Hessel and the Bernheim-Jeune brothers jointly for the sum of 4000 francs. After remaining in their stock for many years, in 1933 *The Library* was sent to New York for exhibition at the Rockefeller Center. Shortly afterwards it was bought by the French State for the Musée du Luxembourg.

A number of writers commented on the unique position Vuillard was in by mid-career to pick and choose the kind of work he enjoyed. In 1910 Sickert admired and envied Vuillard's 'liberty', and in 1914 in his book on modern decorators, Achille Segard talked of Vuillard's freedom 'from all servitude with regard to collectors'. Segard made a distinction between such commercially successful painters as Henri Martin and Gaston Latouche, and Vuillard, who worked for a select few and seemed to be appreciated only by an élite. For Ambroise Vollard, writing in the early 1920s, and Alfred Sutro in the 1930s, Vuillard stood for a certain tradition: he was one of the last representatives of a dying race of true artists who were above commercial considerations and whose only concern was for the betterment of their art. To some extent these characterizations of Vuillard had a basis in fact; he was indeed an artist of high moral scruples, suspicious from very early in his career of easily won success, who aspired to the uncompromisingly high standards of a Mallarmé or a Degas. He was indeed supported by a tight-knit group of select patrons. But this view of him was also part of a romantic myth, comparable to the notion that he disdained to show his work in public. After all, artists have to earn an income to survive and Vuillard was by no means unfamiliar with financial anxieties. Not all of his patrons were 'discerning' and easy to please; and, as his journal reveals, if Vuillard's personal relations with Jos Hessel were always cordial, the attendant rivalry in his business dealings with the Bernheim-Jeune brothers frequently caused awkwardness and strain on both sides.

Such problems notwithstanding, by and large working for the private sector gave Vuillard an enviable

103 *The Villa Les Ecluses at Saint-Jacut.*
1909. Distemper on paper laid down on
canvas, $18\frac{1}{4} \times 18\frac{1}{4}$ in. (46×46 cm.).
Private Collection

freedom to choose his subjects and work in his own way, a freedom unknown to those decorators who served the state. However, it brought frustrations and uncertainties of a different kind, highlighted by the fate of several of the decorative schemes he had painted in the 1890s. Less than two years after Vuillard had completed his third major decorative panel for Jean Schopfer (Plate 41), his client was involved in a ruinous divorce from his rich American wife. She kept the Villeneuve panels (Plates 35, 36) and promptly sold them to Prince Emmanuel Bibesco. Schopfer remarried and kept the third panel in his new apartment in the rue du Bac, but at a later date Vuillard was requested by Schopfer's widow to divide it into two, which involved substantial reworking. Something of the same order befell the large decorations painted for Adam Natanson's dining-room in 1899 (Plates 37, 38). Within a few years the owner died, and they hung for a while in Thadée's apartment before going on semi-permanent loan to someone who, although a great admirer and friend of Vuillard, had neither commissioned nor paid for them – the politician Léon Blum. And again in 1908, when Alexandre Natanson moved house, the nine *Public Gardens* panels (Plates 32, 33), instead of being grouped as an ensemble in a rectangular room, were less satisfactorily hung along a single wall of a long gallery.

Painting a series of decorations for a specific room involved envisaging certain rapports and contrasts – rhythmic and colouristic – within the ensemble. The realization that such a scheme might have a very temporary existence in its intended setting is said to be the reason why Degas refused to undertake this kind of commission. However, Vuillard seems to have accepted the conditions of such mutability – perhaps his début painting décors for the theatre had made him adaptable and accustomed him to the idea of impermanence. In several instances he even welcomed the changes as a chance to make later adjustments to works he no longer found satisfactory.

104 *Beach at Saint-Jacut*. 1909. Distemper on paper laid down on canvas, $26\frac{3}{4} \times 33\frac{3}{8}$ in. (68 × 84.5 cm.). Reader's Digest Association, Inc.

105 *Interrogation of the Prisoner*. 1917. Distemper on paper laid down on canvas, $43\frac{1}{4} \times 29\frac{1}{2}$ in. (110 × 75 cm.). BDIC (Universités de Paris), Musée de l'Histoire Contemporaine

106 *Munitions Factory in Lyons. The Forge.* 1917. One of four subjects from a decorative scheme. Distemper on canvas, 29⅛ × 60⅝ in. (74 × 154 cm.). Troyes, Musée d'Art Moderne (Dépôt des Musées nationaux)

107 *The Sentinel, Gérardmer.* 1917. Pastel on paper, 12½ × 9½ in. (32 × 24 cm.). Private Collection

Working for a particular dealer not only saved Vuillard from the irksome task of chasing up clients for payments, but also cushioned him, to an extent, against the vagaries of the market. Each autumn, after a summer's campaign of work in the country, he would open his studio to Fénéon, who had joined the Bernheim-Jeune firm in 1906. Fénéon had the prerogative to choose for the gallery the best of Vuillard's latest crop. *The Villa Les Ecluses* (Plate 103)and *Woman reading* (Plate 138), for example, both free studies *à la colle* painted in 1909 during Vuillard's summer stay at Saint-Jacut, were acquired in October and went on show in the gallery in November. Sometimes the shows would be supplemented by earlier works that remained unsold or by a newly completed decorative commission prior to its reaching its fixed destination. Thus in 1913, Bernheim-Jeune had the chance to give a preview showing to Vuillard's decorative panels for the Comédie des Champs-Elysées, prior to their installation in the new theatre's foyer. The same exhibition also gave the Paris audience an opportunity to see Vuillard's series of decorative panels destined for the ground floor of the Bernheim-Jeune's summer residence in Normandy.

As well as Vuillard's panels, the decoration of this sumptuous villa at Villers-sur-mer, Bois-Lurette, included pictures by Bonnard, Matisse and others. The villa itself was built in an improbably eclectic Gothic style in a prominent location overlooking the bay. Vuillard embarked on his series of panels in 1911, while staying nearby at Villerville in the Hessels' somewhat less grand villa, Les Pavillons. He continued the following summer during his stay at a villa in Loctudy in southern Brittany. As these were to be light-hearted decorations for a holiday setting, Vuillard's choice of theme, his bright pastel palette and thin and loose handling were entirely appropriate. In the left-hand panel of a door surround (Plate 91) we see Lucy Hessel and Denise Natanson on the veranda at Loctudy. The Paul Poiret toque worn by Lucy was *de rigueur* for the fashionable Parisienne in that summer of 1912, and the modish setting of the veranda (used in many plays at the time), with its coloured glass panels, its floor tiles and its comfortable cane furniture was an equivalent emblem of style. Indeed, Vuillard's decorative scheme as a whole was a vivid testimony to the *douceur de vivre* of the bourgeoisie in an era that was shortly to be brought to an abrupt close by the Great War. When the villa was sold in 1933 the panels were dismantled and substantially reworked.

Vuillard was once again on holiday near Villerville when war was declared in August 1914. Too old at 46 for active service, he was nevertheless mobilized and sent to Conflans to the north-west of Paris; he spent the first four months of the war as *garde voie*, observing the railway line approaching the Gare de Lyon. He was relieved to be released from duty on 12 December. Thereafter Vuillard was able to resume his work more or less as normal, with some limitations. There were to be no further holidays in Normandy for example, fewer exhibitions and few trips abroad. Apart from two visits to Lausanne on family business, Vuillard's only travels were associated with war commissions. He twice made the journey to Lyons, for instance, where Thadée Natanson was administering a munitions factory. Vuillard was commissioned by the owner, Lazare-Lévy, to produce a decorative scheme including painted records of the work being done there, largely by a female workforce. Vuillard's panels thus have a documentary interest. When he visited the factory in March 1917 and was confronted by its brutal shapes, stacks of bombs, heavy lifting gear and machinery, he recorded in his journal: 'flux of sensations – terribly interesting – disordered – feverish'. In the two horizontal panels that were cut down from the original scheme, he represented the factory by day and by night. In one panel (Plate 106) he concentrated on the pearly grey light filtering through the overhead glass and in the other on the more golden light diffused by the hanging electric lamps, producing an overall pattern of shapes and grey tones that was visually intriguing. This alien world of 'engineers, of active, ambitious figures and raging conflicts', as he described it, was a striking contrast to the privileged world of the leisured bourgeoisie that had provided his inspiration hitherto.

108 *Foliage – Oak Tree and Fruit Seller – At the Closerie des Genêts, Vaucresson.* Dated 1918. Distemper on canvas, $74\frac{7}{8} \times 110\frac{1}{4}$ in. (190 × 280 cm.). Chicago, Illinois, Sara Lee Corporation

109 *The Clos Cézanne at Vaucresson.* 1920; reworked 1926, 1935–6. Distemper on canvas, $59\frac{1}{2} \times 43\frac{5}{8}$ in. (151 × 110.7 cm.). New York, The Metropolitan Museum of Art (Wolfe Fund)

110 Photograph by Vuillard of his studio showing the decorative panels for Henri Laroche, *Place Vintimille*, 1917–18. Paris, Antoine Salomon. The three violin-shaped compositions were later reworked in regular rectangular shape. Now in private collections

Vuillard seems not to have considered refusing the request from Clemenceau to go to the front, in early 1917, and make sketches of the combatants, a duty that Jacques-Emile Blanche, for his part, shirked: 'I replied,' wrote Blanche some years later, 'that it seemed irreverent. We the non-combatants would be welcomed as rich ladies are when they set out on works of charity in the slums . . .' Vuillard and fellow artist Paul Baignères spent three weeks with the front line at Gérardmer in the Vosges, Vuillard noting in his journal that their presence caused a certain embarrassment and hostility among the ordinary soldiers. Working in freezing conditions, he filled a sketchbook with rapid notations in pencil and pastel. The sketches bear vivid witness to the cold, discomfort, boredom and tension of existence on the front line, without in any way probing the sensibilities or heroizing the activities of those involved. There are many studies of *The Sentinel* (Plate 107), showing a soldier on look-out duty in the snowy forests, scrutinizing the pine trees for signs of enemy movement. The large commissioned painting *Interrogation of the Prisoner* (Plate 105) was done back in his studio in Paris. Vuillard had witnessed several such interrogations, and where many artists might have exploited the potential pathos and anecdotal interest of the theme, he favoured an understated, even bald documentary approach. His painting projects an image of a typical war-time incident conducted without drama under inglorious circumstances.

During the latter part of the war, Vuillard divided his time between Paris and Versailles. The Hessels had bought a house at Vaucresson, near Versailles, and Vuillard and his mother rented a villa nearby. A surprisingly large number of works date from these years, interiors, portraits and even the occasional decorative panel such as *Foliage–Oak Tree and Fruit Seller* commissioned by George Bernheim (Plates 108, 110, 112, 113), works whose themes appear to give little hint of the troubled world outside. But the

111 Photograph of Vuillard's apartment, rue de Calais, 1917, showing five different versions of his painting *Lucy Hessel reading the Newspaper*. Paris, Antoine Salomon

characteristic blue uniform of the French infantryman crops up in unexpected places, among the congregation seated on the balcony of the *Chapel of the Château of Versailles* for instance (Plate 113), and among the clientèle of the fashionable new tea-room, Le Grand Teddy, for which Vuillard painted an oval decoration (Plate 136). The fox stoles and cloche hats of the three women in the foreground, as well as the design of the tea-room's Art Deco interior with its oriental lighting and lacquer screens, vividly evoke the style of the 1920s. Le Grand Teddy became one of the chic *thé dansants* of the decade, but Vuillard's panel came down with the tea-room's closure in 1930.

The charming group of portraits Vuillard did of his niece Annette Roussel between 1915 and 1917 (Half-title, Plates 80, 101), as she blossomed into an elegant and stylish young woman, came about indirectly as a consequence of war, and seem to symbolize Vuillard's hopes for peace. The hostilities and heavy losses had so perturbed Roussel that he had been forced to retire to a sanatorium in Switzerland, leaving Annette in the care of her grandmother and uncle in Paris. Vuillard also repeatedly reworked a portrait of Lucy Hessel, seated in the warmth and cosy clutter of her rue de Naples boudoir (Plates 111, 112). His obsessive attention to technical problems – to the taut structure of the composition, the multiplication of colours, textures and reflective surfaces – might be seen as symptomatic of the need to take refuge from the horrors of the outside world, to concentrate on an image of reassurance and familiarity. In all the five different states of this contrived and dense composition, the lightest area and focal point remains the open newspaper, a lifeline of information at these critical times.

112 *Lucy Hessel reading the Newspaper, rue de Naples.* 1917.
Distemper on paper laid down on canvas, $41\frac{3}{4} \times 21\frac{5}{8}$ in. (106 × 55 cm.).
Berne, Kunstmuseum

113 *Chapel of the Château of Versailles.* 1917, 1926–8. Distemper on paper laid down on canvas, 37¾ × 26 in. (96 × 66 cm.). Paris, Musée d'Orsay

Chapter Six

VUILLARD AND THE PORTRAIT: THE INTER-WAR YEARS

From about 1912 onwards Vuillard began to take on an increasing number of portraits, and in the last two decades of his life, from 1920 to 1940, his output was dominated by portraiture. Like most painters he had undertaken portraits of an informal kind throughout his career, mainly of members of his family or close friends (Frontispiece, Plates 11, 13, 15). And when he embarked on the series of portraits of his artist friends Maillol, Roussel, Bonnard and Denis (Plates 120, 121) in 1923 he had no fixed client in view. But for the most part his later portraits were formal commissions and, appropriately enough, given Vuillard's established status, his clients tended to be successful in their own right, well-known personalities of stage, literature, politics or medicine. Partly in deference to their standing and expectations but also in keeping with his own interests as a technician, these portraits were brought to a higher degree of resolution than any of his previous work. They involved numerous sittings, were carefully constructed and elaborately prepared, with exhaustive drawings of details and sometimes photographs of the setting. Despite this rather over-involved technique and attention to detail, which repays close scrutiny, many of these late portraits can be found to share the solid sense of design and judicious harmonization of colours of his earlier work.

According to his biographer Claude Roger-Marx, the reason Vuillard accepted so many portrait commissions was to escape the demands of his dealers for repetitions of saleable works. Certainly Vuillard found portraiture a challenging genre, as observations in his journal make clear. No doubt this turning to portraiture was also a consequence of the historical situation, and was not unique to Vuillard. In the uncertain aftermath of the First World War, Vuillard was firmly established in the minds of the picture-buying public as a safe artist, and although he was not one dogmatically to set himself against any new initiatives, he must have felt increasingly alienated by new developments in art. In 1917 he had been drawn into a discussion of the 'sottises picturales actuelles' – 'stupid things going on in painting today', presumably a reference to Cubism – with fellow war artist Paul Baignères, and the violent iconoclastic reaction of the Surrealists, who emerged as the new vanguard movement in Paris in the early 1920s, must have confirmed Vuillard's feelings of distance from the younger generation.

The commission to paint the critic Théodore Duret (Plate 115) in 1912 in a sense marked the beginning of Vuillard's series of late portraits. Mindful of the distinguished artists who had preceded him in the task, he made a point of including Whistler's elegant portrayal of the critic of 1882, *Arrangement in Flesh Colour and Black*, showing Duret in evening dress. It can be seen reflected in the mirror. Vuillard departed from the precedent set by Whistler, and indeed by Manet, of the full-length standing pose against a neutral background and adopted instead a more relaxed pose, with the now elderly critic seated at his desk, surrounded by books, a

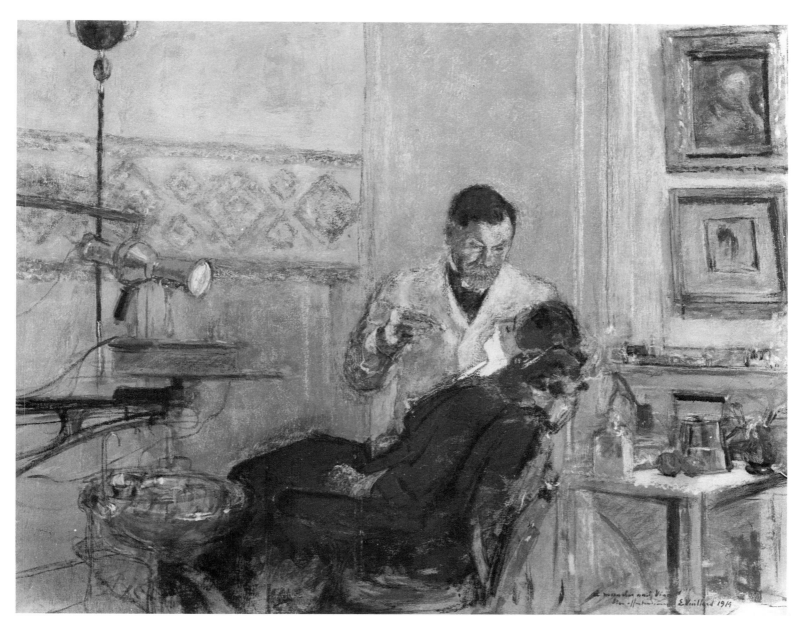

114 *Dr Georges Viau in his Dental Surgery.* Dated 1914. Distemper on canvas, $42\frac{1}{2} \times 54\frac{3}{8}$ in. (108 × 138 cm.). Paris, Musée d'Orsay

115 *Théodore Duret in his Study*. Dated 1912. Oil on cardboard, 37½ × 29½ in. (95 × 74.6 cm.). Washington, DC, National Gallery of Art, Chester Dale Collection

116 *Mme Val Synave in the rue de Calais Apartment.* 1920. Distemper on canvas, $44\frac{1}{8} \times 34\frac{1}{4}$ in. (112 × 87 cm.). Private Collection

cat on his knee. The large scale and *mise-en-page* are strongly reminiscent of Degas's famous portrait of that other key naturalist critic Edmond Duranty, of 1879. However, it was also true to Vuillard's first impressions. After his first meeting with Duret on 4 May 1912 Vuillard noted in his journal: 'Balzacian interior Cousin Pons – pile of books.' Balzac's favourite literary device of using detailed inventories of a setting to indicate the character and habits of its occupant had similarities to the artist's own approach to the portrait. Vuillard was not one to impose himself on his sitters. He was remembered affectionately by his friends for his patience, his selflessness, his willingness to listen and put himself out for others. He would certainly not have subjected his model to the autocratic demands made by a Whistler, or the subjective distortions of a Picasso. Such patience and sensitivity on the part of the portraitist had advantages, especially when the sitter was elderly (Plate 133). The Duret portrait took some two months to complete. During the sittings, Vuillard enjoyed exchanging views with the former champion of the Impressionists about his naturalist ideas. Duret was evidently pleased with the result. He paid Vuillard 2500 francs instead of the 2000 originally agreed.

Vuillard's ability to establish a good rapport with a sitter was often a pointer to a portrait's success. He seems to have been most at ease when he could pose a model in a setting with which he, rather than the sitter, was familiar, be it his apartment or his studio. The 'lamentable story' of the aspiring young actress Lucie Ralph, whom he encountered in 1915 when she had fallen on hard times, evidently moved him. Vuillard's portrait of her (*Lucie Belin*, Plate 60) shows her standing in the cluttered disarray of his boulevard Malesherbes studio, papers, drawings and unfinished paintings stacked behind her. Whereas up until that date, his approach to the portrayal of female sitters to whom he was attracted had tended to be discreet, even elusive (Plates 51, 102), exceptionally here the model is shown full face, in relaxed, open mood, directing her gaze at the artist and smiling. For some years after this, Vuillard took a protective interest in Lucie Ralph's career and provided financial support, to a point where his generosity was in danger of being exploited.

Vuillard's various homages to modern medicine take the form of direct and documentary working portraits. His *oeuvre* includes several portraits of doctors in consultation with patients, in the surgery, the hospital ward or at the patient's bedside. His friend Dr Henri Vaquez remained one of Vuillard's most loyal patrons. He helped Vuillard out of an awkward situation by acquiring three panels of the place Vintimille, which the artist had begun to paint in 1917 for Henri Laroche in the form of violin-shaped rococo '*trumeaux*' (Plate 110). He also commissioned works on his own account around this time, portraits of himself and of his wife. When Vuillard painted *Dr Vaquez at the Hôpital de la Pitié* (Plate 123) in 1921, he typically opted to portray the doctor on his daily ward rounds, accompanied by his younger assistants Luterbacher and Parvu, as he paused to talk to a female patient and allay her fears. Vuillard enlivened the somewhat clinical pale green, cream and white tonality of the hospital interior with a warmer, more colourful view through the window on to the garden. It is a sober, respectful yet tender image, quite distinct from the usual run of melodramatic medical and surgical paintings produced during the nineteenth century, by Toulouse-Lautrec among others.

A number of Vuillard's portraits of around 1920–5 not only include but self-consciously refer to other art. The presence of art objects and pictures on the walls of an interior had never escaped his attention. Back in the mid-1890s he had painted a conversation piece showing the apartment of Paul and Marie Ranson, where regular early Nabi meetings were held (Plate 9). A number of stridently coloured Nabi paintings hang on the blue walls, notably Sérusier's portrait of *Ranson in Nabi Costume* of 1890, on the top right, partially cut off by the picture frame. Vuillard's painting is especially valuable because it is the only visual record of such meetings. In his post-1900 interiors, when he habitually paid even greater attention to detail, Vuillard frequently made it possible to identify specific works hanging on the walls. In *Lucy Hessel in the Small Salon, rue de Rivoli* (Plate 57) of 1903–4, for instance, one recognizes paintings by notable contemporaries, independent artists whose

117 Sketch for the portrait of *Mme Val Synave*. 1920. Pencil on paper, 8⅜ × 4¾ in. (21.2 × 12.3 cm.). Private Collection

work Jos Hessel was just beginning to promote: a small version of Cézanne's *Bathers* hangs centrally over the doorway, Denis's *Three Young Princesses* or *Chivalric Legend* of 1893 is immediately above Lucy Hessel's head, and Lautrec's *Femme de maison* of 1893 (now in the Norton Simon Collection) hangs beside it on the adjoining wall. Perhaps the irony of this oddly inappropriate juxtaposition amused Vuillard. In *The Visit* (Plate 90), an interior painted thirty years later, Vuillard represented the now more opulent cabinet in the Hessels' rue de Naples apartment. Other than the large Bonnard *Au Grand Lemps* on the wall, the paintings by Vuillard's contemporaries are less in evidence than the various small oriental figures that were presumably more recent additions to the Hessels' collection. Even in his painting of the surgery of his friend the dentist Dr Viau (Plate 114), a documentary record of a dental examination in a clinical environment, Vuillard could not resist noting the pictures owned by this amateur collector; among the group of works on the wall to the right hangs a portrait by Eugene Carrière.

This habit of showing pictures within pictures was surely not simply an example of Vuillard's all-embracing vision but had a more active purpose. It enabled him to pinpoint, even pay homage to his sitter's tastes. On other occasions it allowed him to make ironic combinations of forms and themes and was a way of gently poking fun. In the portrait of the woman painter *Mme Val Synave* (Plate 116) of 1920, executed in Vuillard's salon-studio in the rue de Calais, the juxtaposition of the sitter's buxom, uncorseted profile with the ideal classical proportions of the plaster cast Venus de Milo torso was hardly fortuitous. Was this perhaps

118 *Self-Portrait with Prints in the Cabinet de Toilette, rue de Calais.* 1923–4. Oil on cardboard, 32 × 25 in. (81 × 67 cm.). New York, Ian Woodner Family Collection

119 *The Painter K.-X. Roussel in his L'Etang-la-Ville Studio* (Final Version). 1934–7. Distemper on paper laid down on canvas, 48⅞ × 44 in. (124 × 112 cm.). Musée d'Art Moderne de la Ville de Paris

120 Sketch for the *Sculptor Maillol* panel. 1923.
Pencil on paper, 6⅛ × 5⅜ in. (15.5 × 13.7 cm.).
Private Collection

Vuillard's tongue-in-cheek allusion to Mme Val's own Renoiresque paintings? What is certain, thanks to a journal entry for 21 December 1917, is that he was well satisfied with this compositional arrangement: 'afternoon Val Synave, hesitation which makes me anxious; nudes, jewels, "clinquant" [glitter], cold features; decide on a pleasing effect in front of the Venus de Milo, anxiety overcome.' Having firmly established the pose and arrangement in a small pencil drawing (Plate 117), Vuillard was to leave the project in abeyance for some two years before he came back to it. The *Mme Val* portrait, like that of *Lucy Hessel reading the Newspaper* (Plate 112), gives a compressed sense of space but makes use of a mirror, that favourite device of portraitists since the time of Ingres, to add to the visual interest and spatial ambiguity. The inclusion of a richly coloured tapestry gives the right-hand section of the composition textural and colouristic richness.

The plaster cast of the Venus de Milo had pride of place on Vuillard's mantelpiece (Plate 111), as Thadée Natanson fondly remembered, dwarfing the small Maillol terracottas and delicate Tanagra figurines with which it co-existed. This jumbled collection of sculpture, drawings and reproductions, where a Degas pastel of a dancer adjusting her hair ribbon vied for attention with a reduced-scale cast of the Capitoline *Antinous*, testifies to the breadth of Vuillard's tastes. The disproportion of the objects clearly intrigued him and he used the mantelpiece as the subject of one of his overdoor panels for the *At the Louvre* decorative scheme (Plate 125). The seemingly haphazard composition which includes only the lower abdomen of the Greek goddess seems deliberately to avoid all classical principles of symmetry and balance, although its theme harked back to similar overdoors by Chardin depicting the Attributes of the Arts.

The last of all Vuillard's decorative schemes for private clients, the *At the Louvre* series – painted between 1921 and 1922 (Plates 125–7) – was destined to remain in its intended setting in Basle for some forty

121 *The Sculptor Aristide Maillol at Marly-le-Roi* (Maquette). 1923. Distemper on paper laid down on canvas, $45\frac{5}{8} \times 45\frac{1}{2}$ in. (116 × 115.5 cm.). Musée d'Art Moderne de la Ville de Paris

122 *The Game of Bridge – The Salon at the Clos Cézanne, Vaucresson.* 1923. Distemper on canvas, 39³⁄₈ × 30 in. (100 × 76 cm.). Private Collection

123 *Dr Vaquez and his Assistant Dr Parvu at the Hôpital de la Pitié*. Dated 1921. Distemper on canvas, 55⅞ × 52 in. (142 × 132 cm.). Paris, Académie Nationale de Médecine

years. The attention to physiognomy, the slightly smaller scale and the tighter handling of paint set these panels apart, in some measure, from Vuillard's earlier decorative schemes, and reflect his painstaking preparatory drawings and pastels. He may again have had in mind the inescapable example of Degas (such as his etchings and paintings of women looking at art in the Louvre), or even the enigmatic figure of Gabriel de Saint-Aubin, who was in many ways a precursor with his minutely detailed drawings of eighteenth-century picture displays. The Louvre theme had a personal interest for Vuillard. In the four larger panels he represented some of his favourite haunts in the museum, where he had spent so many hours studying and copying works of art. The Salle La Caze housed a nineteenth-century collection of eighteenth-century masters which had captivated him since his student days. In Vuillard's panel (Plate 127) one can clearly make out a portrait by Largillière, a Chardin still life, a Fragonard study of a girl and a Watteau nude. The model for the member of the public who appears on the lower right was Annette Roussel and in the *Salle Clarac* panel (Plate 126) she is joined by her fiancé, the young artist Jacques Salomon, who was to become one of Vuillard's most devoted admirers. In the 1920s the Salle Clarac was mainly devoted to sculpture and decorative arts; the glass cases seen in Vuillard's painting contained examples of ceramics and Tanagra figurines. Vuillard made use of the verticals, horizontals and diagonals of the setting to construct a tight grid-like composition. He also

124 Jacques-Emile Blanche: *Walter Richard Sickert*. 1935. Oil on canvas, 31¾ × 24¼ in. (80.5 × 61.5 cm.). Manchester City Art Gallery

125 *Venus and Statuettes, Vuillard's Mantelpiece.* Dated 1922. One of two overdoor panels for the *At the Louvre* series. Distemper on canvas, 17¾ × 45¼ in. (45 × 115 cm.). Private Collection

adopted a low, oblique viewpoint, similar to that of his two main figures, thereby directly involving us as spectators with their experience of looking at art. In view of the fact that the *At the Louvre* scheme was executed in the aftermath of the First World War, it can almost be seen as a reassertion of faith in France's great artistic heritage.

The delightfully informal *Self-Portrait with Prints in the Cabinet de Toilette* (Plate 118) provides another example of this witty use of art within art. There can be little doubt that Vuillard intended to point up the ironic similarity between the venerable profile of the Prophet Zacharias (his photograph of the Michelangelo appears pinned to the wall on the lower right) and his own now balding head and whitened beard. Above the Michelangelo photograph are reproductions of the flower-gatherer from a Roman wall painting and of Le Sueur's *Raymond Diocrès speaking after his Death*, one of a series of panels in the Louvre by the seventeenth-century painter, whom Vuillard greatly admired. On the wall to the left are three Japanese prints, including, in the centre, one of Hiroshige's *Hundred Views of Edo*. These then were some of the works of art with which Vuillard chose to surround himself, works that formed his daily intimate environment even as he performed the mundane ritual of washing his hands after work.

Few paintings show more clearly how imbued Vuillard was with the tradition of everyday life painting in seventeenth-century Holland than his almost monochrome painting of his elderly mother entering his bedroom (Plate 130), a picture which was given the title *The Housewife (La Ménagère)*, presumably with Vuillard's approval, at his major retrospective exhibition in 1938. Painted in 1925 it was one of the last pictures of the rue de Calais apartment. His mother, stooped but still active and houseproud, is shown dressed in black. The room's musty greys and browns, its antique chair, lamp and collection of black and white pictures on the wall call to mind Terborch or Vermeer. The picture also seems an echo of Vuillard's earlier Symbolist interiors, a deliberate contrast in expression to the bright, electrically-lit modern interiors he was so often called upon to paint at this time, or indeed to the exuberantly decorative garden picture he had painted of *The Clos Cézanne at Vaucresson* (Plate 109) two years before, which shows an unexpected affinity with late Monet. The move from the rue de Calais in 1926 and the death of his mother in 1928 marked the end of an era for Vuillard. From his new apartment in the place Vintimille he recorded the successive disappearance of the various floors of the rue de Calais block in photographs and pastel sketches, as demolition workers moved in. In a journal entry for

126 *Ceramics* or *Display Cases in the Louvre. The Salle Clarac.* Dated 1922. Distemper on canvas, 38¼ × 45½ in. (97 × 115 cm.).
Private Collection

127 *Painting in the Louvre. The Salle La Caze*. Dated 1921. Distemper on canvas, 63 × 51¼ in. (160 × 130 cm.).
Private Collection

February 1928, he noted how he had tried, unsuccessfully he felt, to capture the brilliance of a sun effect on the scene: 'living rays of sun on the old façades; street in shadow; cubist poster to cap it all and traces of apartments on the wall.'

During the last decades of his career, Vuillard's critical reputation rose or fell according to his success as a portraitist. The hazards of professional portraiture had first been highlighted by Walter Sickert, with reference to Vuillard and Jacques-Emile Blanche. In his review of the 'International Society' exhibition in London, published in *The New Age* in 1910, Sickert had drawn a distinction between, on the one hand, the artist who was a free agent (Vuillard) and on the other the professional portrait-painter (Blanche), always at the mercy of his client. Sickert contrasted the lively humour and wit of Vuillard's paintings, which revealed an artist who was master of his client and in no way encumbered by professionalism, with the conscientious interior drawing-rooms of Blanche, which he judged to bear the mark of the professional portraitist: 'Every touch bespeaks them painted for the owners of the rooms. Livery is an honourable wear, but liberty has a savour of its own.' Although painted some years later, Blanche's portrait of his friend Sickert (Plate 124) exemplifies his approach.

Sickert's comparison prompts one to ask whether in fact Vuillard was always able to maintain his 'liberty' once he embarked on commissioned portraits. In 1928 André Lhote, for one, wrote disparagingly in *La Nouvelle Revue Française* of Vuillard's recent portrait of the writer Jean Giraudoux (Plate 128), which was on show at an exhibition entitled 'Portraits of Today' organized by Claude Roger-Marx. Unlike the Cubist portraits by Picasso, shown in the same room, which succeeded in suggesting the sitter's inner life, Vuillard's, he felt, did no more than give an exterior resemblance. In his obituary of Vuillard in 1941, Lhote judged him to have been too pliant before the whims and vulgar tastes of a client, for losing that envied independence and autonomy. Vuillard, like Blanche, was often required to set the model in a room he or she owned (Plates 131, 132, 133, 134). Indeed, in his portrait of the celebrated writer Anna, Comtesse de Noailles (Plate 131), who had already been painted by Blanche, as indeed had Giraudoux, Vuillard represented her in bed where, like her friend and contemporary Marcel Proust, she did her writing (Plate 135). Such was Vuillard's reputation for exactitude that when he arrived for the first sitting the Comtesse apparently instructed her maid to clear away the jars of vaseline from her bedside lest they find their way into the picture too. Lhote condemned the portrait for its 'vulgar colours', and for the 'blinding reality' of its roses and fabrics, which he considered a 'triumph of . . . bad taste'. He was referring as much to the taste of the sitter as to that of the artist in faithfully recording the details of the floral wallpaper and embroidered satin bedspread.

André Lhote's criticisms cannot simply be brushed aside, although his views were undoubtedly partial, coloured by his own artistic standpoint: as a painter he adhered to the principles of Cubism which he practised in a disciplined, tempered, Cézanne-inspired form within the continuing native French tradition of classicism. He thus opposed what he saw as Vuillard's unselective realism. Lhote, an influential figure in the mid-war years, both as a writer and as a teacher, suspected that it was on the strength of such opulent society portraits as *Anna de Noailles* that Vuillard had finally been admitted to the Institut in 1937, only three years before his death. It is undeniable that Vuillard took on certain commissions from people he scarcely knew with reluctance, and found their execution correspondingly tedious and unsatisfactory. He would never shirk his responsibilities or take short cuts, adopt formulaic poses for instance, as had been the practice of so many portraitists in the past, and for that very reason his scrupulous honesty and attention to minutiae could become somewhat laboured.

A diverting account was left by Marie-Blanche, Comtesse de Polignac, a talented musician and prominent figure of *le beau monde* in the 1920s and 30s, of the experience of sitting to Vuillard. The portrait

128 *Jean Giraudoux at his Desk*. 1926. Pastel on paper, $19\frac{1}{2} \times 25\frac{3}{4}$ in. (49.5 × 65.5 cm.). Private Collection

129 *Vuillard's Room at the Château des Clayes.*
c. 1933. Distemper on paper laid down on canvas,
30¾ × 39½ in. (78 × 100.5 cm.). Art Institute of
Chicago

130 *Mme Vuillard in the Artist's Bedroom, rue de
Calais.* 1924. Oil on cardboard, 17⅞ × 11¾ in.
(43.5 × 29.8 cm.). Richmond, Virginia Museum of
Fine Arts, Mr and Mrs Paul Mellon Collection

131 Study for the *Portrait of
Anna de Noailles*. 1931.
Charcoal on canvas,
43¼ × 49¾ in. (110 × 126 cm.).
Paris, Musée d'Orsay

(Plate 134) was commissioned by her mother, Jeanne Lanvin, the successful couturière, whom Vuillard also painted, portraying her at work in her smart business premises (Plate 132). Although the Comtesse de Polignac's portrait was begun in 1928, Vuillard seems not to have finally completed it *à la colle* until 1936. The setting was a house in Neuilly and Vuillard asked the sitter to pose in her bedroom, decorated in blue and white chintz. He wanted no tidying up to be done; the clutter of accessories was to be faithfully painted in, much to the delight of the Comtesse, who was convinced that Vuillard had recognized the sentimental importance these objects had for her. The sittings continued daily over a long period, each session lasting maybe no more than twenty minutes; sometimes Vuillard would bring a small sketchbook and make drawings in pencil or pastel of details: the Comtesse's ear, the convolvulus, the nose of her lapdog. By this stage, Vuillard would already have established his overall composition in pastel, although in the final portrait he set the Comtesse further back into her room, with the unfortunate result, according to one critic, that she appeared as though viewed through the wrong end of a telescope, engulfed by her belongings. In his drawing practice, Vuillard differed from more conceptual draughtsmen such as Delacroix or Bonnard. Rather than repeatedly rehearsing and revising an overall design, he made one small sketch, which usually sufficed to fix it; and the large bulk of his drawings were made of details, to build up a dossier of documentation to fill in that scaffolding. While he worked, or afterwards at lunch, the Comtesse evidently engaged Vuillard in conversation. She recalled with delight the variety and modest erudition of his remarks and regretted not having kept a record of them.

It would be enlightening to know what Vuillard himself felt about the role of portraitist. He frequently noted his difficulties, dissatisfactions and anxieties about art in his journal. And he was clearly alert to debates

132 *Mme Jeanne Lanvin in her Office*. 1933. Distemper on canvas, 49 × 53¾ in. (124.5 × 136.5 cm.). Paris, Musée d'Orsay

about the contemporary artist's role in society. He took note of the heretical notion voiced by more than one writer in the 1920s that the revolution in taste introduced by the naturalists and Symbolists had been in the long term harmful. In December 1923, he copied out statements by Edmond Jaloux and Guglielmo Ferrero. The gist of their thinking was that the hard-won liberty to paint any subject whatever, the overturning of the traditional repertoire by the Impressionists and their followers, had brought in its train a number of disadvantages for the artist. At a time when Vuillard himself had retreated from the role of avant-garde painter and opted for a more secure, restricted relationship with a steady clientèle, some of Ferrero's statements may have seemed directly pertinent. In the past, Ferrero argued, 'rules governing art, precise to the point of pedantry, were not the only things that tyrannized the slave of the pen, the brush or the chisel. Religion, the State, the caprices and interests of the dominant and moneyed classes placed limitations on the free reign of his genius . . . but this servitude was not without certain advantages [in that the artist knew where he stood, what was required] . . . the floor of his prison was solid . . .' Today, however, the artist could 'do whatever he wants, but he has to invent everything: subjects, style, technique; he is continually obliged to produce something new without ever being sure of being understood or ever knowing with what yardstick he will be measured.' It is difficult to know to what extent Vuillard agreed with Ferrero's views, for he made no personal observations. But the very fact that he copied them down suggests they had given him food for thought. He certainly believed that as a result of the rapid turnover of opposing 'isms' there had been a woeful loss of direction in contemporary art and criticism, and that artistic success had become simply a matter of luck. If an artist remained true to his convictions he would have to harden himself against wild fluctuations in taste and critical response.

133 *Mme Adrien Bénard in her Salon.* 1928–9. Distemper on canvas, 45 × 40⅜ in. (114.5 × 102.5 cm.). Paris, Musée d'Orsay

134 *Marie-Blanche, Comtesse Jean de Polignac in her Bedroom.* 1928–32. Distemper on canvas, 45¼ × 34⅝ in. (115 × 88 cm.). Paris, Musée d'Orsay

The companion portraits of his four old friends and comrades-in-arms, Bonnard, Denis, Roussel and Maillol, absorbed much of Vuillard's attention in the early 1930s. The portraits seem to have been intended simultaneously to pay homage to their achievements and to draw attention to their contrasting methods. We are given rare glimpses of the artists at work, out of the public eye – for instance Roussel (Plate 119) in his chaotic, gloomy, laboratory-like studio at Etang-la-Ville, and Maillol (Plate 121) busy working on the *Monument to Cézanne* in the dusty garden annexe of his Marly studio. The origin of the scheme seems to date back to a sketch of Maillol at work made in the summer of 1923 (Plate 120). All four portraits and their accompanying maquettes, in some ways fresher and more spontaneous than the finished works, were bought by the Petit Palais and exhibited at the Universal Exhibition in 1937.

Alongside his steady output of portraits, Vuillard continued to produce still lifes, interiors and landscapes, particularly during the holiday periods when he stayed with the Hessels. At their house near Vaucresson, the so-called 'Clos Cézanne' because it had been bought on the proceeds of the sale of a Cézanne, there were evening games of bridge (Plate 122). At the Château des Clayes, a magnificent country property which the Hessels acquired in 1926, they and their guests could play the role of aristocrats. Vuillard was allocated his own bedroom, painted in Bonnard-like yellows, in which he evidently delighted. His large late interior (Plate 129) is of particular interest since it records Vuillard's work in progress on the walls. It is also visually bold and exciting, orchestrating space into a flattened pattern of geometric shapes just as in some of his most daring synthetist interiors of the 1890s. The park and garden, laid out by Le Nôtre, inspired many of Vuillard's late landscapes and provided the bucolic setting for his last decorative works such as the *Comedy* panel at the Théâtre de Chaillot (Plate 137), and the mural for the Palais des Nations in Geneva.

135 Sketch for the *Portrait of Anna de Noailles: Right Hand holding a Pen*. 1931. Pencil on paper, 8⅛ × 5¼ in. (21 × 13.2 cm.). Private Collection

Chapter Seven

CONCLUSION

The major event of Vuillard's final years, apart from his election to the Institut in 1937, was the retrospective of his *oeuvre* at the Pavillon de Marsan in 1938. Just as he had had to be urged by friends such as Denis to accept the honour of election to the Institut, it had needed considerable persuasion to get him to sanction this ultimate accolade. The exhibition comprised over 300 works, in all media, the majority lent from private collections. The occasion prompted him to retouch quite a number of earlier pieces. Allowing for some probable inaccuracies of dating, it is interesting that between a third and a half of the works shown came from the period before 1900. Was this the result of expediency, or a reflection of the taste of the times? Or did Vuillard himself, who was consulted over the selection and presumably took a keen interest in the exhibition representing his life's work fairly, consider the early years to have been the period of his most varied artistic achievements?

The retrospective and the accompanying show of works from 1890 to 1910 at Bernheim-Jeune's prompted a number of tributes. Pierre Véber, for instance, left a moving testament to his friendship with Vuillard. For Maximilien Gauthier, writing in *L'Art Vivant*, the message of Vuillard's work was a comforting one in troubled times and his remarks nicely counteract those made earlier by Lhote: 'His [Vuillard's] portraits are mysteriously animated by an intense interior life and most of his compositions are delicate hymns to the goodness of living at home, that's to say within limits, within those four walls where each one of us is master, capable of creating a better world.' However, the times were scarcely propitious for Vuillard's achievements to receive the attention they deserved. War with Hitler's Germany was unmistakably looming, despite the moment of optimism that had accompanied the election of the first-ever Socialist Popular Front administration, under the premiership of Vuillard's old friend Léon Blum, in 1936. As the Comtesse de Polignac recorded, Vuillard still adhered to the radical views of his youth, and believed that Blum's election heralded a new and better age. According to Thadée Natanson, Vuillard's sympathies had always been with the poor and he rejoiced to see Blum's Matignon Accords of 1936 bring subtantial gains in social and labour conditions for the working classes.

Vuillard's commitment to peace, and to the concept of the League of Nations, found artistic expression in 1938 when he was commissioned to paint a monumental mural for the Palais des Nations in Geneva. He felt the context demanded an allegorical subject and he turned to Le Sueur once more, relying heavily on his example to cope with the unaccustomed demands of flying figures and classical draperies. Although a courageous undertaking, it was one of his least characteristic decorations.

The failure of the Popular Front administration, the outbreak of war in 1939 and the rapid capitulation of both the French armies and the French Republic were devastating blows from which Vuillard never recovered. With Lucy Hessel at his bedside, he died in La Baule, at the age of 71, on 21 June 1940.

If for us Vuillard's painted world still carries that message of optimism noted by Gauthier, in the context of his *oeuvre* as a whole his development in the 1920s and 1930s of an art of minutiae must stand as a complete reversal of the rigorous instructions he had given himself in 1890. Under the spell of Nabi doctrine, he had set aside the faithful noting of details in pursuit of the goal of synthetic expression. Was this a contradiction, or was there a consistent trend underlying Vuillard's career? In his first still lifes, and in his journal, notes and sketches, he had shown himself to be an artist who was not only sensitive to the nuances of colour, light and shade, but greedy for sensation, alert to humorous detail, quick, lively and absorbed in the pageant of modern life. We have seen how painfully he worked through the reductive lessons of the Symbolist aesthetic, controlling his receptive vision; having absorbed them he was able to relax and return to the more expansive view of nature that came naturally. Today we are coming to understand and enjoy Vuillard's later works, although his early paintings, with their simplicity and poised edge of uncertainty and tension, and his major decorative panels, with their broad vision and exquisite harmonies, are still regarded as his greatest achievement.

136 *'Le Grand Teddy' Tea-Room*. 1918–19; reworked from 1930. Distemper on oval canvas, 59 × 114⅛ in. (150 × 290 cm.). Geneva, Petit Palais, Oscar Ghez Foundation

137 *Comedy*. 1936–7. Decoration for the Théâtre de Chaillot. Distemper on canvas, 132 × 138 in. (335 × 350 cm.). Paris, Palais de Chaillot

NOTES

Notes to sources referred to in text
For full references see Select Bibliography

Chapter One

Page

10 *Journal*, November 1908.

12 *Journal* (carnet 1 1888–90).
    Journal, after 20 Nov. 1888, p. 12r.

18 Meeting with Véber, *Journal*, 4 Dec. 1888, p. 22r.
    Letter from Sérusier to Denis, undated but datable to summer 1888.
    Sérusier, 1950, p. 40.

Chapter Two

Page

22 *Journal* (carnet 2 1890–1905), September 1890, p. 19v.

28 Letter from Denis to Sérusier, Serusier, 1950, p. 49.
    Journal (carnet 1), 7 Sept. 1890, p. 55v.
    Letter from Ranson to Verkade, early July 1892; see G. Mauner, 1978, p. 280.

36 R. Marx, 'Notules d'Art', *Le Voltaire*, 1 Oct. 1892.

40 *Journal* (carnet 2), July–Aug. 1894, pp. 45v–47v.

44 Letter from Bonnard to Vuillard, undated, reprinted in part in *La revue blanche*, exhibition catalogue, 1983, p. 12.

49 J. Schopfer, 'L'Art moderne et les Académies', *La Revue Blanche*, 13, July–Sept. 1897, pp. 358–62.
    R. de la Sizeranne, 'Puvis de Chavannes', *Revue des Deux Mondes*, November 1898; reprinted in *Puvis de Chavannes*, exhibition catalogue, Paris and Ottawa, 1977, p. 197.
    Segard, 1914, p. 263

Chapter Three

Page

56 G. Mourey, 'Studio-Talk: Paris', *The Studio*, XVI, 74, 15 May 1899, pp. 281–2.
    T. Natanson, 'Une Date de l'histoire de la peinture française', *La Revue Blanche*, 18, 1899, p. 511.
    Denis, March 1899; I, 1957, p. 150.
    Denis, Feb. 1898; I, 1957, pp. 133–41.

60 Segard, 1914, p. 255.
    Natanson, 1948, p. 375.
    Signac, *Journal inédit*, 16 Feb. 1898; see J. Rewald, ed., 1952, p. 277.

61 For Vuillard's remarks about Le Vésinet, see Denis, Nov. 1901; I, 1957, p. 176.

64 Vaillant, 1974, p. 54.

68 'Collection Thadée Natanson: Désignation des tableaux: Vente 13 juin 1908', in J. Halperin, ed., 1970, p. 258 (catalogue notes probably compiled by T. Natanson).
    P. Valéry, *Eupalinos ou l'Architecte*, first pub. 1921; *Oeuvres 11*, Paris 1960, p. 84.

69 T. Bernard, 'Jos Hessel', *La Renaissance*, XIIIème année, no. 1, Jan. 1930.

72 Vaillant, 1974, p. 97.
    A. Gide, 'Promenade au Salon d'Automne', *Gazette des Beaux-Arts*, 1905, p. 480.
    F. Monot, 'Salon d'Automne', *Art et Décoration*, 1905, p. 200.

73 Denis, April 1906; II, 1957, p. 36.
    O. Mirbeau, 'L'Art et le ministre', *Le Journal*, 15 April 1900; reprinted in *Des Artistes*, vol. 2, 1913, pp. 95–6.

76 Ludovici, 1926, p. 135.
    W. Lewis and L. Fergusson. *Harold Gilman. An Appreciation*, London 1919, p. 19.
    Blanche, 1921, p. 281.
    Sickert, 'Vuillard and Jacques Blanche', *The Art News*, 10 Feb. 1910; 'The Post-Impressionists', *The Fortnightly Review*, Jan. 1911; 1947, pp. 269–70, 108.

Chapter Four

Page

77 Lugné-Poe, I, 1931, pp. 243–72.
    W. Rothenstein, *Men and Memories*, vol. 1, London 1931, p. 90.
    A. Symons, *Plays, Acting and Music*, London 1928, p. 25.

78 C. Roger-Marx, 'Paul Fort et le Théâtre d'Art', *Comoedia illustré*, 1913.
    P. Quillard, 'De l'inutilité absolue de la mise en scène', *La Revue d'Art dramatique*, 1 May 1891; see Robichez, 1957, p. 188.
    A. Pepperall, 'Symbolism as Reflected in Vuillard's Interiors', unpublished BA Thesis, University of Manchester, 1980.

84 For Lugné's London Tour, 25–30 March 1895, see Robichez, 1957, pp. 326–33.
    A. Sutro, 1933, p. 18

88 A. Jarry, *L'Art Littéraire*, Jan.–Feb. 1894, p. 21; quoted in Robichez, 1957, p. 247.
Journal (carnet 2), 7 Nov. 1894, pp. 54, 55v.

96 For discussion of Bernstein's *Israël* see Bissell, 1930.

97 Vaillant, 1974, p. 96.
Robichez, 1957, p. 295.

98 M. Guillemot, 'La Décoration du Théâtre des Champs-Elysées', *Art et Décoration*, XXXIII, 1913, pp. 111–12.
P. Géraldy, *Féeries* (evocations of J. Giraudoux and E. Vuillard), Paris 1946, pp. 18–19.

Chapter Five

Page
104 See for example Steinlen's illustration 'Graine de marlous' from his album *Dans la vie*, Paris 1901.
Journal, Dec. 1909.

108 Wilson Bareau, 1986.

110 For Vuillard's relations with Proust see above and I. Dunlop, 'Proust and Painting', in P. Quennell, ed., 1971, pp. 120–3.

114 I am grateful to Gloria Groom, Assistant to the Curator of European Painting, Art Institute of Chicago, for providing details about Miss Chapin from the doctoral thesis she is preparing for the University of Texas, 'Painting as Decoration for the Domestic Interior: Vuillard and his Patrons, 1892–1912'.
Hommage à 'Commerce', exhibition commemorating the literary review founded by Marguerite Chapin, Rome 1960.
Journal. Between November 1910 and April 1911, references passim.
Journal, 4 Oct. 1911.
Sickert, 1947, p. 270.
Segard, 1914, p. 254.
Vollard, 1937, p. 372.
Sutro, 1933, pp. 26–7.

119 *Journal*, 17 March 1917.

122 Blanche, 1939, pp. 31–2.

Chapter Six

Page
126 C. Roger-Marx, 1946, p. 20.
Journal, 15 Feb. 1917.

130 *Journal*, 4 May 1912.
Journal, 1 June 1915.

134 *Journal*, 21 Dec. 1917.
Natanson, 1948, p. 372.

142 *Journal*, 3 Feb. 1928.
Sickert, 1947, p. 269.
A. Lhote, 'Les Arts: Portraits d'aujourd'hui', *n r f*, Feb. 1928, p. 276.
ibid., 'E. Vuillard', *n r f*, March 1941, pp. 501–2.
de Polignac, 1965, pp. 135–42.

147 Edmond Jaloux, quoted in *Journal*, 23 Dec. 1923.
Guglielmo Ferrero, quoted in *Journal*, 22 Dec. 1923.

150 R. Coolus, 'Le Château des Clayes', *La Renaissance*, XIIIème année, no. 7, July 1930.

Chapter Seven

Page
151 For Véber, 1938, see Russell, 1971, pp. 99–100.
M. Gauthier, "Exposition", *La Vivant*, 1938, nos. 219; 220.
Natanson, 1948, pp. 373–4.

PHOTOGRAPHIC ACKNOWLEDGEMENTS

The works of Edouard Vuillard, Jacques-Emile Blanche and Ker-Xavier Rousel are © DACS 1988. The work of Pierre Bonnard is © ADAGP, Paris and DACS, London 1988.

Copyright A. C. L. Bruxelles 33; © 1988 The Art Institute of Chicago. All Rights Reserved. L. L. and A. S. Coburn Fund, Martha E. Leverone Fund, Charles Norton Owen Fund and anonymous Restricted Gift 37. Gift of Mr and Mrs Leigh B. Block 129; Photo Michael Tropea 139; Photograph Galerie Vallotton 51; Reproduced by Courtesy of the Trustees of the British Museum 29, 30; © Christie's Color Library 122; Photo Courtesy of the Lefevre Gallery 57; By Courtesy of the Board of Trustees of the Theatre Museum 22; Felton Bequest 1955 58; Room of Contemporary Art Fund 1943 59; Photo David Heald 72, 73; Lynton Gardner Photography, New York 118; All Rights Reserved. Metropolitan Museum of Art. Gift of Alex M. Lewyt 6. Wolfe Fund, 1952, Catherine Lorillard Wolfe Collection 109; Gift of Fletcher Steele 13; © 1988 Sotheby's Inc. 78; Wildenstein & Co. New York 69; Huguette Berès, Paris 107; Archive Bernheim Jeune 86; Photo Bulloz 42, 43; Cliché des Museés Nationaux, Paris 5, 12 ,28, 32, 34, 40, 45, 76, 89, 100, 113, 114, 131, 132, 133, 134; Studio Lourmel, Photo Routhier, Paris 8, 9, 10, 11, 15, 20, 24, 31, 60, 64, 88, 101, 105, 116, 128, 137: Cliché Museés de la Ville de Paris 119, 121; Chester Dale Collection 90; © Prolitteris, Zurich 112.

SELECT BIBLIOGRAPHY

Monographic studies

A. Chastel, *Vuillard 1868–1940*, Paris 1946.

L. Oakley, *Edouard Vuillard*, The Metropolitan Museum of Art, New York 1981.

S. Preston, *Vuillard*, New York 1971, London 1985.

C. Roger-Marx, *Vuillard. His Life and Work*, London 1946.

C. Roger-Marx, *L'Œuvre gravé de Vuillard*, Paris & Monte Carlo, 1948.

J. Salomon, *Vuillard, témoignage*, Paris 1945.

J. Salomon, *Auprès de Vuillard*, Paris 1953.

J. Salomon, *Vuillard admiré*, Lausanne 1961.

J. Salomon, *Vuillard*, Paris 1968.

Articles

R. Bacou, 'Décors d'appartements au temps des Nabis', *Art de France*, IV, 1964, pp. 190–205.

A. Chastel, 'Vuillard et Mallarmé, *La Nef*, 26, Jan. 1947, pp. 13–25.

J. Dugdale, 'Vuillard the Decorator', *Apollo*, 36, Feb. 1965, pp. 94–101; 68, Oct. 1967, pp. 272–77.

C. Frèches-Thory, '*Jardins Publics* de Vuillard', *Revue du Louvre*, 4, 1979, pp. 305–12.

T. Leclère, 'Edouard Vuillard', *Art et Décoration*, 226, Oct. 1926, pp. 97–106.

C. Roger-Marx, 'Portrait de Vuillard', *Formes*, March 1932, pp. 240–1.

J. Salomon and A. Vaillant, 'Vuillard et son Kodak', *L'Oeil*, 100, April 1963, pp. 14–25, 61.

J. Wilson Bareau, 'Edouard Vuillard et les princes Bibesco', *Revue de l'Art*, 74, 1986, pp. 37–46.

U. Perucchi-Petri, *Bonnard und Vuillard im Kunsthaus*, Zurich 1972.

Exhibition catalogues

Exposition E. Vuillard, Musée des Arts Décoratifs, Pavillon de Marsan, Palais du Louvre, May–July 1938.

A. Carnduff-Ritchie, *Edouard Vuillard*, The Museum of Modern Art, New York 1954, reprint 1969.

Bonnard, Vuillard et les Nabis (1888–1903), Musée National d'Art Moderne, Paris, June–Oct. 1955.

Edouard Vuillard, Ker-Xavier Roussel, exhibition catalogue by P. Georgel, Orangerie des Tuileries, Paris 1968.

J. Russell, *Vuillard*, introduction, catalogue and extracts from important selected texts by Vuillard's contemporaries, London 1971.

General

J-E. Blanche, *Propos de Peintre: De David à Degas* (preface by Marcel Proust), Paris 1919.

J-E. Blanche, *Dates*, Paris 1921.

J-E. Blanche, *Portraits of a Lifetime (1870–1914)*, London 1937.

J-E. Blanche, *More Portraits of a Lifetime (1918–38)*, London 1939.

M. Denis, *Journal*, 3 vols. 1884–1943, Paris 1957.

A. Gold and R. Fizdale, *Misia*, London 1980.

G. Guisan and D. Jakubec, eds, *Félix Vallotton: Documents pour une biographie et pour l'histoire d'une oeuvre*, vol. 1, Lausanne 1973.

J. Halperin, ed., *Félix Fénéon: Oeuvres plus que complètes*, Tomes I & II, Geneva 1970.

A. Ludovici, *An Artist's Life in Paris and London*, London 1926.

G. Mauner, *The Nabis, their History and their Art (1888–96)*, Columbia University thesis, 1967; Garland, 1976.

T. Natanson, *Peints à leur tour*, Paris 1948.

T. Natanson, *Un Henri de Toulouse-Lautrec*, Geneva 1951.

M-B. de Polignac, 'Edouard Vuillard, souvenirs', from

Hommage à Marie-Blanche Comtesse Jean de Polignac (limited private publication), Paris 1965.

M. Proust, *A la Recherche du temps perdu*, Paris 1954.

P. Quennell, ed., *Marcel Proust – A Centenary Volume*, London 1971.

La Revue Blanche, 1889–1903. 30 vols. Reimpression, Geneva 1968.

La Revue Blanche, exhibition catalogue with introduction by G. Bernier, Wildenstein, New York, Nov.–Dec. 1983.

J. Rewald, ed., 'Paul Signac, "Extraits du journal inédit"', *Gazette des Beaux-Arts*, vol. 36, July–Sept. 1949, pp. 97–128; vol. 39, April 1952, pp. 265–84.

A. Segard, *Peintres d'aujourd'hui: Les Décorateurs*, 2 vols. Paris 1914.

P. Sérusier, *A B C de la peinture*, with correspondence, Paris 1950.

W. Sickert, *A Free House! or The Artist as Craftsman* (collected writings and articles), London 1947.

A. Vaillant, *Le Pain Polka*, Paris, 1974.

A. Vollard, *Souvenirs d'un marchand de tableaux*, Paris 1937.

E. Weber, *France, fin de siècle*, Cambridge, Mass. and London 1986.

Theatre

C. Bissell, *Les Conventions du théâtre bourgeois contemporain en France*, Paris 1930.

C. Frèches-Thory et al., *1913 Le Théâtre des Champs-Elysées*, Les Dossiers du Musée d'Orsay, Paris 1987.

A. Lugné-Poe, *La Parade*, 4 vols. Paris 1931–46; 1, *Le Sot du tremplin*, Lettres-Annexe, pp. 243–72, includes letters to Lugné-Poe from Paul Fort, Bonnard and Denis; 2, *Acrobaties*, both Paris 1931.

J. Renard, *Journal 1887–1910*, Dijon 1960.

J. Robichez, *Le Symbolisme au théâtre*, Paris 1957.

A. Sutro, *Celebrities and Simple Souls*, London 1933.

138 *Woman reading in the Reeds, Saint-Jacut.* 1909 Distemper on paper laid down on canvas, $17\frac{1}{2} \times 25\frac{3}{8}$ in. (44.5 × 64.6 cm.). Cambridge, Fitzwilliam Museum

INDEX

139 *Sketch for Coquelin Cadet*. 1890. Watercolour, $8 \times 5\frac{1}{8}$ in. (20.5 × 13 cm.).
Chicago, Dr Martin Gecht